MW00627855

DIARY COMICS

JANUARY 2010
to
SEPTEMBER 2012

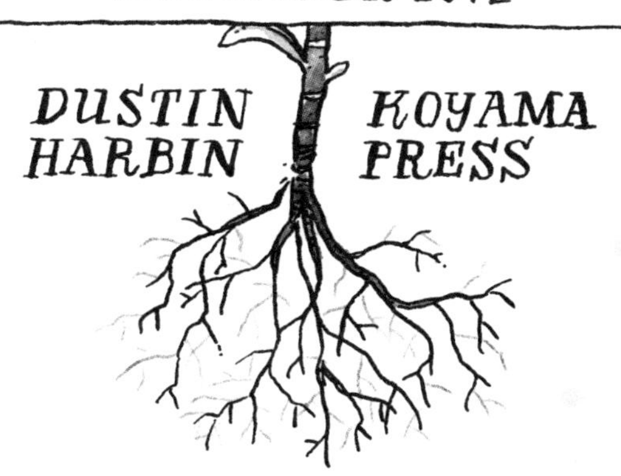

DUSTIN HARBIN

KOYAMA PRESS

DHARBIN.COM

THESE STRIPS ARE REPRODUCED AT ROUGHLY ORIGINAL SIZE. I'VE LEFT MANY ERRORS IN PLACE TO PRESERVE THAT ORIGINAL ROUGHNESS. THANKS TO MY EDITORS FOR THEIR PATIENCE IN ALLOWING THIS PECCADILLO.

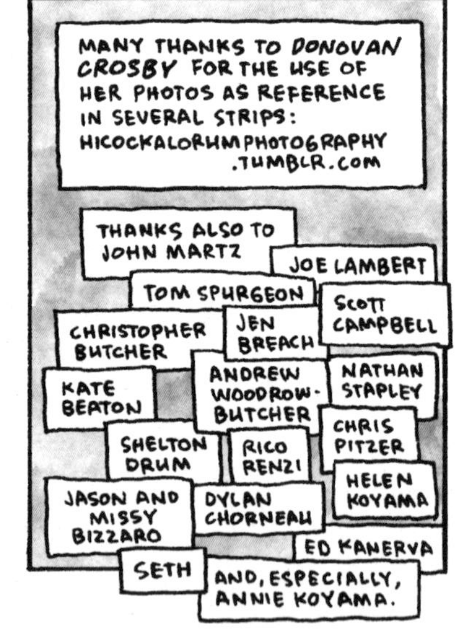

FOR KATE,
OF COURSE.

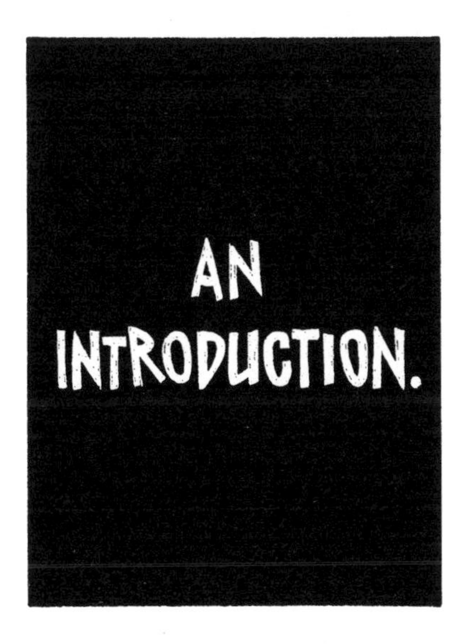
AN INTRODUCTION.

IMAGINE A TRAIN,
HEADED EAST OR WEST.

THE TRAIN HAS MANY CARS.

SOME ARE OLD AND DENTED AND RUSTY. THE ONES TOWARD THE BACK LOOK NEWER, BUT THEY ALL HAVE THAT TRAIN DIRT.
CHRGA CHRGA

MOST OF THE CARS ARE EMPTY.

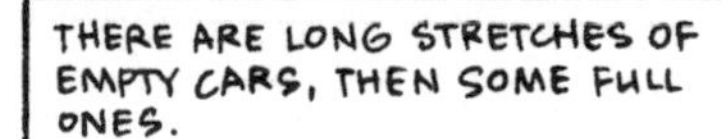
THERE ARE LONG STRETCHES OF EMPTY CARS, THEN SOME FULL ONES.

OR MAYBE JUST ONE OR TWO.

IT'S HARD TO TELL WHERE THE TRAIN IS GOING. YOU CAN SEE THERE ARE MOUNTAINS.

OR MAYBE TREES.

MAYBE NEITHER.

IN 2010 I STARTED MAKING DIARY COMICS ON NEW YEAR'S DAY, IN A LITTLE 4"x 5" NOTEBOOK.

THEY WERE HOURLIES AT FIRST.
WHAT'S DHARBIN DOING?

I REMEMBER THINKING AT THE TIME--
IT'S HARD TO HAVE FUN WHEN I HAVE TO KEEP PAUSING...

...TO DECIDE HOW TO DESCRIBE THE FUN.

WHICH -- LOOKING BACK NOW -- HAS BECOME A MAJOR THEME FOR ME.

BOTH IN MY WORK AND MY LIFE.

THERE'S A THING CALLED THE "*OBSERVER EFFECT*," OFTEN CONFUSED WITH HEISENBERG'S UNCERTAINTY PRINCIPLE --

ESSENTIALLY, YOU CAN'T MEASURE SOME THINGS WITHOUT CHANGING THEM.

YOU SEE WHERE I'M GOING, RIGHT?

OBSERVING THE MOMENT CHANGES THE MOMENT.

NOT ONLY THAT, IT ROUNDS ALL THE CORNERS AND SHARPENS ALL THE CURVES.

IT MUSHES THINGS INTO A YOU-SHAPED SHAPE, FITS IT INTO A YOU-SHAPED SPOT IN YOUR BRAIN, AND MOVES ON.

IS THAT BAD?

YEAH, PROBABLY.

BUT MAYBE--MAYBE--
JUST UNTIL YOU NOTICE
THAT THAT'S WHAT
YOU'RE DOING.

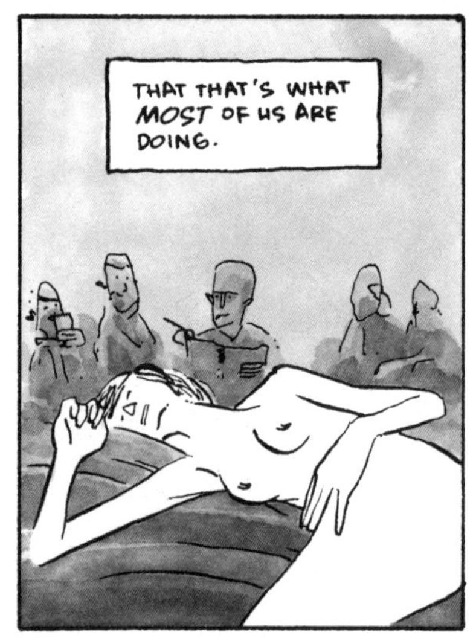
THAT THAT'S WHAT
MOST OF US ARE
DOING.

YOU'RE NOT INSIDE A
STORY, YOU ARE A STORY.

A STORY THAT MAY
OR MAY NOT END
WHEN YOU DIE.

THE MOMENTS YOU WERE PART OF ARE STILL THERE, BUT YOU ARE GONE.

WHAT STORY WILL GO
ON WITHOUT ME WHEN
I'M GONE?

PROBABLY NOT THE
ONE I'VE TOLD
MYSELF

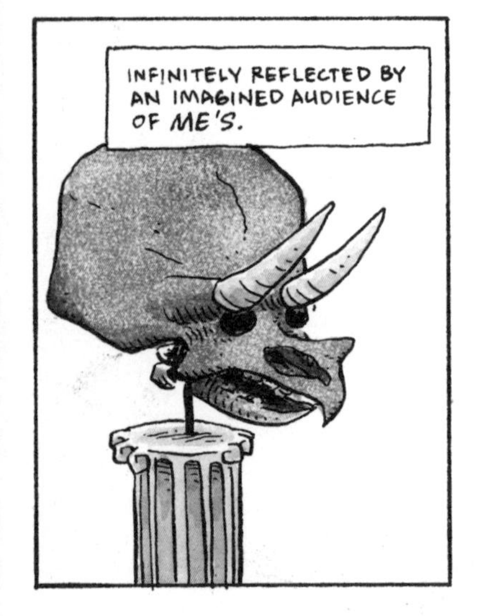
INFINITELY REFLECTED BY
AN IMAGINED AUDIENCE
OF ME'S.

I'D LIKE TO THINK IT WILL
BE MORE INTERESTING
THAN THAT, BUT OF COURSE
I'LL NEVER KNOW.

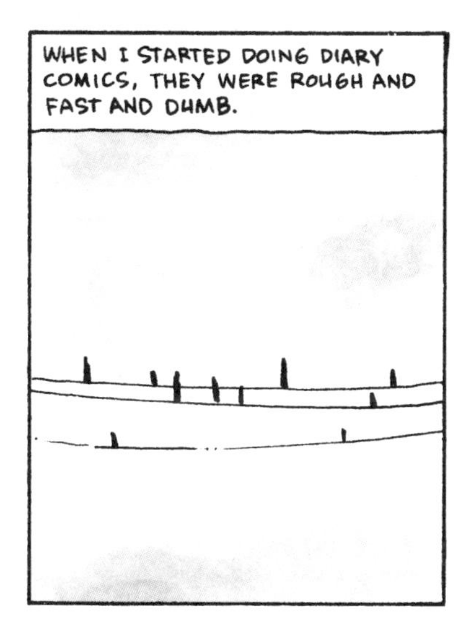
WHEN I STARTED DOING DIARY COMICS, THEY WERE ROUGH AND FAST AND DUMB.

I WOULD DO ONE FOR EACH DAY, USUALLY SELECTING A MOMENT THAT SEEMED WORTH SHOWING.

AS I STARTED IMPROVING THE QUALITY OF THE DRAWINGS, THE QUALITY OF THE MOMENTS I CHOSE STAYED THE SAME.

HECK, USUALLY I WAS STRUGGLING TO REMEMBER WHAT HAPPENED ON A GIVEN DAY.

REMEMBER THE TRAIN?
IMAGINE YOU'RE RUNNING
ALONG THE TOP OF IT.

AT THE SAME SPEED
AS THE TRAIN.

BUT IN THE OPPOSITE
DIRECTION.

IMAGINE YOU'RE
MOVING AT ALL.

TELLING MYSELF MY OWN STORY IS VERY DANGEROUS.

ESPECIALLY BECAUSE I KNOW *YOU'RE* THERE, AND I CAN'T HELP TELLING YOU, TOO.
BLAM!

IT'S EASY TO GET INTO A RECURSIVE LOOP AND LOSE ANY CONTACT WITH PERSPECTIVE.

AUTOBIOGRAPHY MAKES IT EASIER THAN EVER TO BE BORING AND LAZY.
BLAP!

IT TOOK ME NEARLY TWO YEARS TO REALIZE THAT.

IT WAS PAINFUL AND EXHILARATING.

I HOPE YOU'LL FORGIVE ME FOR TAKING SO LONG.
SPLAT!

OH MAN NEW YEAR, GOT TO
THESE DIARY COMICS BEGAN AS AN EXERCISE,

BECAME A DAILY RECORD,

THEN A CRUTCH AND AN OBLIGATION

BUT FINALLY TURNED INTO SOMETHING I WAS VERY PROUD OF.
DUSTIN, DINNER IS NO PLACE FOR METAPHORS!

SOMETHING I FELT HAD VALUE OUTSIDE OF ITSELF, SOMETHING THAT WOULD LEAVE SOME RIPPLES BEHIND IT.

AND SOMETHING OF *PERSONAL* VALUE AS WELL,

BOTH AS THERAPY, AND AS CRUCIBLE

AND AS A PLACE I CAN GO TO THINK.

I'M A CREATIVE PERSON WHO'S RARELY SURE WHAT HE'D LIKE TO CREATE.
CHRGA CHRGA

SO IN THE MEANTIME I CREATE THIS, AND BY EXTENSION, MAYBE JUST A LITTLE BIT, MY
OH GIVE ME A BREAK

I HOPE YOU FIND IT USEFUL, AS I HAVE.
ALTHOUGH IF YOU DON'T, I'LL LIKELY NEVER KNOW.

AND THAT IS AS IT SHOULD BE.
SEP 2014

10
01 JAN -- 7.00 AM
BEEP BEEP
OH MAN NEW YEAR, GOT TO START IT RIGHT
HRR, WAKE UP DIHARB

10
01 JAN -- 8 ISH AM
UH-OH

10
01 JAN ~~04~~ - - 6.21 PM
IMPROMPTU DANCE PARTY WHILE WAITING FOR CORRECT CHILD/ADULT RATIO

10
01 JAN ~~04~~ - - 7.05 PM
WE DID NOT WAIT LONG ENOUGH.
I WANT TO PLAY
IS IT MY TURN
YOU'RE DOING IT WRONG
STOMP
STOMP

02 JAN 10 -- 12.16 AM
DANG I SHOULD BE AT HOME ALREADY...

02 JAN 10 -- 12.27 AM
A REALIZATION
HOW IN THE WORLD CAN I DO THESE HOURLIES EVERY DAY?

6 JANUARY 2010 6:30 PM
"SUDDEN HIGH DEMAND"
OH MAN HOCKEY SOUNDS GOOD BUT I TOLD KATE I'D GO HAVE A DRINK..

6 JANUARY 2010 6.50 PM
HM KATE HAS TO WORK LATE -- I COULD GO TO THE HOCKEY GAME, OR WORK OUT, OR GET SOME WORK DONE...
TAP TAP
TAP TAP

BUT:
6 JANUARY 2010 8:30 PM
PEW PEW PEW

7 JANUARY 2010 12.30 AM
GOING TO BED UNDER NEW FLANNEL SHEETS

7 JANUARY 2010 9.59 PM
UH-OH LOOKS LIKE I DO HAVE TO TEACH THAT COMICS CLASS--
CRAP I'D BETTER FIGURE OUT WHAT TO SAY..
TOUCH

8 JANUARY 2010 1:30 PM
"TEAM WORKOUT"
MY DOG DRAGS HIMSELF AROUND ME IN CIRCLES WHENEVER I DO CRUNCHES.
HRF/
HUF

8 JANUARY 2010 5.00 PM
AT AMELIE'S BAKERY
TEA MAKES OLD LADIES TALK SUPER LOUD.
AH BLAH BLAH
BLAH BLAH
BLAH
BLAH

9 JANUARY 2010 8.11 AM
GOT OUT OF BED 90 MIN. LATE, HAVE CLASS SOON, WON'T HAVE TIME FOR BREAKFAST--
BUT SOMEHOW SEE FIT TO DO THIS COMIC?
WTF

12 JAN '10 7.15 PM
I KEEP GETTING DISTRACTED FROM WHAT DIETER'S EXPLAINING BY THE WAY HIS BEANIE IS MAKING HIM EASY TO IMAGINE AS A CAR-TOON.

12 JAN '10 9.53 PM
THAT REALLY DOES LOOK LIKE DIETER! I'M THE BEST!

13 JAN '10 9.33 AM
"OVERSLEPT"
WHY DOES 2 HOURS EXTRA SLEEP ALWAYS MEAN 200% MORE TIRED??

13 JAN '10 ~~11.01 PM~~ 3.00 PM
FELT DEPRESSION COMING ON, DID 100 CRUNCHES TO STAVE THAT SHIZZ OFF.
IT WORKED, TOO!
DRAGGING IN CIRCLES

13 JAN '10 8.15 PM
COOKING FOR ONE IS LONELY WORK.
HM HOW MUCH GARLIC DO I PUT IN HERE?

13 JAN '10 11.30 PM
FORTUNATELY I NEVER SLEEP ALONE.
Z Z Z
Z Z Z

14 JAN '10 7.15 AM
YAWNNNN

14 JAN '10 9.30 PM
LETTERING WITH A CROW QUILL FOR FIRST TIME:
SWEET.

17 JAN '10 8.30 AM

18 JAN '10 10.30 AM
"NOT FEELING IT"
I HATE THIS $!#@ COMIC!
KLIK
KLIK

18 JAN '10 2.30 PM
"STILL NOT FEELING IT"
I HATE THIS $!!&?!# ILLUSTRATION, TOO!

18 JAN '10 3.30 PM
"UH-OH"
I HATE TRYING TO RELAX BY DRAWING OUTSIDE!

21 JANUARY '10 2.30 PM
APPARENTLY CREDIT UNIONS ARE WHERE IT'S AT.
OKAY, SO WHAT ARE THE FEES WITH THAT ACCOUNT?
OH WE DON'T CHARGE FEES
!
BANK LADY
CHOICE BALLOON PLACEMENT!

21 JANUARY '10 3.45 PM
"I SURE AM GLAD THESE CHURCH TYPES ARE HAVING THEIR MEETING AT MY TABLE"
YES AND THE SPIRIT AND THE UH-HUH AND SOME PEOPLE
OH MY YES THE SPIRIT THAT'S MY FAVORITE I LOVE IT SO

21 JANUARY '10 4.45 PM
"DON'T FORGET THE CELLPHONES!"
OH YEAH BRO YOU DEFINITELY SHOULD WORK OUT IN THE MORNINGS--
I'LL PROBABLY MAKE VP BY SUMMER...

22 JANUARY '10 6.30 PM
"ACTUALLY GETTING STUFF DONE TODAY"

24 JANUARY '10 11.30 PM
WORKING LATE AS HUGE DOWNPOUR OUTSIDE GOES ON...
PSSHH
GREAT NIGHT MUSIC
PSSHH

25 JANUARY '10 1.00 PM
THE LONGER I WORK ON A STRIP, THE LESS ANY-ONE WILL GIVE A CRAP ABOUT IT.
I COULD SPEND 20 MINUTES ON A STRIP ABOUT FALLING DOWN AS A KID AND PEOPLE WOULD FLIP THOUGH...

25 JANUARY '10 5.00 PM
WALKING THE DOG IN THE WIND

25 JANUARY '10 9.30 PM
AT SKETCH CLUB
ANIDA IS MAKING FUN OF MY "AWAY" WORK SETUP.
WHAT?

26 JANUARY '10 10.30 AM
SCANNING THESE DIARY COMICS TAKES LONGER THAN DRAWING THEM
BRRZZZ

26 JANUARY '10 11.30 AM
AW, SICK DOGGIE
BUDDY YOU NOT FEELING GOOD?
AW, LIL BUDDY..

26 JANUARY '10 3.30 PM
YOU CAN TELL THE DOG'S NOT FEELING GOOD WHEN HE LETS THE CAT GET IN MY LAP WITH HIM.

26 JANUARY '10 10.55 PM
LOST SEASON 5 FINALE
BLUBBER
WHEEZE
SNIFF

01 FEBRUARY 10 2.25 PM
THE BECHTLER MUSEUM

01 FEBRUARY 10 2.45 PM
CHARLOTTE IS GETTING PRETTIER
KLIK!

HEY CHIEF--
HEY CHIEF JUST DON'T PHOTOGRAPH THE ART NOW OKAY?
HA-HA, NO JUST THIS VIEW
OKAY CHIEF
CHIEF?

01 FEBRUARY 10 3.15 PM
THE MAIN EXHIBIT
FWOOSH

01 FEBRUARY 10 3.30 pm
VIVE LE CORBUSIER

?
?

01 FEBRUARY 10 4.10 pm
FULL OF IDEAS

01 FEBRUARY 10 5.00 pm
THIS BUS IS BROKEN
PUSH
UM
PUSH
SNORT

12 FEBRUARY 10 3.30 PM
MADE IT TO MEETING ON TIME, BUT HE WAS HALF-HOUR LATE
SORRY I'M LATE
I'M SICK
HA-HA NO BIGGIE

12 FEBRUARY 10 8.30 PM
DINNER WITH KATE
YOU KEEP PUTTING ME INTO YOUR COMICS, I HAVE TO WATCH WHAT I SAY NOW
DON'T WORRY I CAN'T DRAW YOU ANYWAY

12 FEBRUARY 10 10.45 PM
A BETRAYAL!
OKAY I LOCKED THE DOOR NOW
SPLUT!
HEE HEE

12 FEBRUARY 10 11.15 PM
SNOWBLIND
SORRY, I CAN'T SEE ANYTHING--WHAT'S THAT LAST BEER THERE?
"ROGUE"
OH, YES I LIKE ROGUE, ONE OF THOSE

26 FEBRUARY 10 9.30 AM
OVERSLEPT. OOPS
WAIT IS THE 6 UPSIDE DOWN? WHY IS THE 6 UPSIDE DOWN?
BEE
BEE
BEE

26 FEBRUARY 10 3.45 PM
SHIPPING RICHIE RICH FRAME
SO IF I SHIP IT REGULAR, IT MIGHT NOT GET TO L.A. BY NEXT FRIDAY?
RIGHT
BUT IT MIGHT?
WELL
WHAT DO YOU THINK?
UM
FRAGILE
FRA-GILE
FRAGILE
FRAGILE

26 FEBRUARY 10 4.30 PM
WORKING ON CLASS NOTES
I SHOULD HAVE EATEN SOONER; I'M CATCHING A BUZZ

26 FEBRUARY 10 7.20 PM
FRIDAY NIGHT DARK

27 FEBRUARY 10 11.30 AM
THE MOST IMPORTANT LESSON
LAST WEEK OF WINTER COMICS CLASS--
REMEMBER: THE DRAWING IS THE LEAST IMPORTANT PART.

3.30 PM
STILL STRUGGLING

9.30 PM THERE SHOULD BE GRAMMIES FOR BEATLES ROCK BAND
I COULDN'T DAN
WITH ANOTHER
WOOO!!
WHEN I SAW HER STAND THERE

11.10 PM THE BIZZAROS THROW THE BEST KITCHEN PARTIES, FOR SURE
AW HER
ANDING
HERE
WOO

MARCH 10 THURSDAY
A PENIS PROBLEM AT KUNG FU!
UT!
I THINK MY WILLY CAME OUT OF MY UNDERWEAR!

HM, ER
SURREPTITIOUS FUMBLING

WHEW! GETTIN INTO ANYTHING CRAZY THIS WEEKEND?
SHE MUST KNOW!
SHE KNOWS!

OH, HA-HA
WELL YOU KNOW ME...
SURREPTITIOUS FUMBLING

8 MARCH 10 STILL MONDAY
SKETCH CLUB WHINETIME
...AT LEAST THERE'S AN ARTS COMMUNITY FOR YOU GUYS IN CHARLOTTE..

THERE'S PRACTICALLY NO ONE IN CHARLOTTE TO TALK CARTOONING WITH

IN PORTLAND, EVEN THE CHIMNEY SWEEPS MAKE COMICS ON THE SIDE...

ALL MY PEERS IN COMICS LIVE INSIDE OF MY COMPUTER

8 MARCH 10 MONDAY!
A RELAXING PRE-SPRING DAY
I SHOULD WORK OUTSIDE WHILE THE WEATHER'S SO GOOD
PERFECT FOR RELAXING
HUSH BUDDY...
RELAX LIKE ME!
BARK
BARK
AW BUDDY DON'T ROLL IN THAT-- EWW
JUST RELAX
R-RELAX BUDDY
RELAX
BARK
BARK

15 MARCH 10 MONDAY SKETCH CLUB LIKENESS CONTROVERSY!
I MEAN LET'S FACE IT-- YOU DRAW WOMEN ALL THE SAME--
IT'S TRUE, YES

YOU JUST NEED TO ACCENTUATE WHAT'S DIFFERENT--
LIKE, I HAVE HEAVY EYELIDS. YOU COULD USE THOSE--

BUT ANIDA--
YOU CAN'T DRAW SOMEONE WITH DOTS FOR EYES AND ACCENTUATE THEIR EYELIDS.
HMF

BESIDES. NO ONE ON THE INTERNET REALLY KNOWS WHAT YOU GUYS LOOK LIKE ANYWAY
WELL THAT'S TRUE

18 MARCH 10 THURSDAY
ANIDA'S WEIRD DREAMS
DO YOU EVER HAVE NIGHTMARES ABOUT ANIMALS HAVING SEX?
UM

ISN'T IT WEIRD?
WELL

COS THEY JUST DO IT--
THEY'RE TO THE POINT!
SSPLRRBBT

THEY'RE NOT TRYING TO BE STYLISH
#91

25 MARCH 10 THURSDAY
THE MOST EMBARRASSING MOMENT OF MY THIRTIES (TO DATE):
EXCITED ABOUT THE SCOTT PILGRIM MOVIE, I LINKED TO THE NEW TRAILER ON TWITTER.

1 APRIL 10 THURSDAY
"DHARBSTARTER"
I WAS UP LATE SO I SET UP A **KICKSTARTER** FUND TO PRINT A COLOR NEWSPAPER COMIC.

8 APRIL 10 THURSDAY
OREOS: BY JOE WEIDER
I'VE BEEN TRYING TO GAIN MUSCLE WEIGHT LATELY.

SOMETIMES I GET REALLY GUNG HO AND WORK OUT TWICE IN ONE DAY, DOING WEIGHTS IN THE AFTERNOON...

...THEN KUNG FU AT NIGHT.
UT!
H-HUT

BUT THEN GORGE MYSELF ON OREOS AFTER DINNER.
...AND ONE AND TWO
35
#111

9 APRIL 10 FRIDAY
HUNGRY LIKE THE DHARB
I HAVE A CRUSH ON THIS ONE WAITRESS AT THIS ONE RESTAURANT.

BUT TONIGHT SHE'S ALL BLOTCHY IN THE WAY YOU GET AFTER YOU'VE BEEN CRYING A WHOLE LOT.
SNF
SNRF

LOOKS LIKE BOYFRIEND TROUBLE.

D
35
#112

11 APRIL 10 SUNDAY
BLUES FOR BLACK CAESAR
I'VE BEEN TRYING HARD NOT TO FALL INTO A FUNK
YOW YOW YOW YOW

BUT MY CAT IS SICK--HE'S NOT EATING AND HE SMELLS FUNNY AND HE'S CONSTANTLY DRINKING WATER AND PEEING.
YOW YOW

THE INTERNET THINKS IT'S DIABETES--
YOW YOW YOW YOW YOW

SOMETIMES THE FUNK JUST HAPPENS, IT'S NOT ALL JUST BRAIN CHEMISTRY--
YOW YOW YOW YOW YOW

14 APRIL 10 WEDNESDAY
MOWW?
TALKING TO THE VET ABOUT MY SICK CAT:
SO DO YOU HAVE ANY PROBLEM WITH NEEDLES?
... NO?

SINCE HIS KIDNEYS ARE SICK, WE HAVE TO HYDRATE HIM ANOTHER WAY...
MOWR?

SO NOW I HAVE TO DO THIS EVERY TWO DAYS--
--AND THE IV DRIPS 150 ML OF FLUID RIGHT INTO HIS BACK!
MOWW

AND IT COMES TO $415.62. VISA?
MOWW
TELL ME ABOUT IT, KITTY.
#116

19 APRIL 10 MONDAY
INTRIGUE AT CASA DEL NEIGHBOR
SO IN THE MORNING MY NEIGHBORS' DOOR WAS STILL OPEN. #HMMM

I KEPT IMAGINING FACES PEEKING OUT OF THE DARK STRIPE.

OR WORSE.

FINALLY, THAT NIGHT, I TOOK ACTION!
Hey Hank--
Your door is open.
--DUSTIN HARBIN

20 APRIL 10 TUESDAY
THE SETUP
MY NEIGHBORS CAME BY TO THANK ME (?) FOR WATCHING THEIR... DOOR.
WELL I GUESS
GRRRR
BUDDY LATER SNAPS AT MIRIAM

TURNS OUT IT HAD JUST BEEN LEFT OPEN ACCIDENTALLY, BUT SUDDENLY THE CONVERSATION CHANGED--
SO DUSTIN
ARE YOU SINGLE? I HAVE A FRIEND I WANT YOU TO MEET
ALARM

SHE'S ONE OF THE NUDE MODELS AT OUR FIGURE DRAWING GROUP.
HMM
AND SHE'S BEAUTIFUL AND QUIRKY AND YOU GUYS WOULD GET ALONG GREAT!
QUIRKY, HUH?

MIRIAM, IS THIS GIRL A HIPPIE?
MAYBE
YES
#12

21 APRIL 10 WEDNESDAY
GETTING BETTER
I'M GETTING BETTER AT MY LETTERING ON CASANOVA.
ESPECIALLY THE BOLD LETTERS.

BUT LORD, THESE RAPIDOGRAPHS.

22 APRIL 10 THURSDAY
I'M ALSO GETTING A LOT BETTER AT KUNG FU.
YES!
HRK!

I WISH IT DIDN'T HURT SO MUCH TO BE A BADASS.

28 APRIL 10 WEDNESDAY
THE ONE THING
ME AND ANIDA AND OUR FRIEND BO WERE HAVING DRINKS AND TALKING ABOUT RELATIONSHIPS--
OKAY, NAME ONE ABSOLUTE MUST FOR YOU--

EASY-- HE'S GOTTA HAVE A SENSE OF HUMOR.
WHAT ABOUT YOU, DUSTY?
SHE'S GOTTA BE EXCITING!

BO?
JUST ONE THING? WHAT IF I PICK THE WRONG ONE?
IT'S JUST US, BO..

IS IT BAD IF I SAY "GOOD-LOOKING?" DOES THAT SOUND WEIRD?
NO THAT'S FAIR
SURE HA-HA
35
#127

4 MAY 10 TUESDAY
THE ENQUIRER DHARBIN
I WAY UNDERESTIMATED THE TIME IT WOULD TAKE TO LAY OUT MY NEWSPAPER.
UH-OH

BUT I HAD FORGOTTEN HOW PLEASANT IT IS TO WORK ON PRINT DESIGN--
... AND A 3/16" GUTTER, INCREASED BY 15%, LET'S SEE HERE

I LOVE THE EXACTITUDE OF PRINT-- THESE PIXELS WILL ALL TURN TO INK I CAN TOUCH AND SMELL.
R DHARBIN
I FEEL LIKE MY MIND IS UNIQUELY SUITED TO IT.

I FEEL LIKE MY DAD MUST WHEN HE BUILDS A CABINET. IT'S STRONG AND EXACT AND FUNCTIONAL WORK.
LEADING
GUTTER
3/16"
QUARTER INCH
PLUMB LINE
STYL
PALET
CHISEL
KERNING
ROUTER BIT
LIVE AREA
#132

12 MAY 10 WEDNESDAY
DHARBIN YOU HAVE FORGOTTEN
MONTH AGO DHARBIN, I CAN'T REMEMBER WHAT HAPPENED IN MAY ANYMORE TO MAKE COMICS ABOUT!

YOU SHOULD HAVE TAKEN BETTER NOTES!
UH, YOU SHOULD'VE TAKEN BETTER NOTES!

13 MAY 10 THURSDAY
GUYS WE'RE ON THE SAME TEAM
LIKE, WHAT HAPPENED ON MAY 13TH? ANYTHING? YOU DON'T KNOW!
HEY!
WHERE DID OUR MUSCLES GO??
I WORKED HARD ON THOSE TCAF MUSCLES!

!!
35
#147

17 MAY 10 MONDAY
MYSTERY CONVERSATION
IN MY NOTES FOR TODAY, I WROTE (A MONTH AGO) "KATE CONVO."
BUT WHAT THE HECK DOES THAT MEAN?

I'M PRETTY PRIVATE (FOR SOMEONE WHO DOES LIKE 8 DIFFERENT AUTOBIO COMICS), SO THERE ARE ONLY CERTAIN THINGS I'D INCLUDE IN A STRIP.
SO I HID THE BODY UNDER THE FLOORBOARDS
!

NOR WOULD I INCLUDE ANYTHING THAT WOULD EMBARRASS KATE -- GUYS, THAT'S JUST NOT MY STYLE--
MY FAVORITE BAND IS BLUES TRAVELER!
!!

ODDS ARE, ANYTHING TRULY INTERESTING WOULD NEVER MAKE IT INTO THIS STRIP AT ALL -- MY PLEDGE TO YOU!
PLOP
#151

5 JUNE 10 SATURDAY

DON'T FACEBOOK ME, BRO

LATE NIGHT, WE RETIRED TO ME AND **JOE LAMBERT**'S HOTEL ROOM AND POLISHED OFF NEIL BRAMLETTE'S ***MOONSHINE***

BUT LATER, BEFORE WE ALL BROKE UP FOR THE NIGHT, HE SAID SOMETHING THAT BLEW MY BRAIN UP A LITTLE--

YOU NEED TO GET YOUR SHIT TOGETHER AND DO SOME ***REAL*** COMICS--

YOU SHOULD BE PITCHING TO **MOME**.

MY VOICE WAS SHOT, BUT SUNDAY AFTERNOON I MODERATED A PANEL ON **AUTOBIO COMICS**.

ALL 3 OF THESE GUYS ARE IN ***UPWARDLY MOBILE*** PHASES OF THEIR CAREERS, A PHASE I AM **HUNGRY** FOR.

I'M ***FASCINATED*** AND ***REPELLED*** BY THE IDEA OF AUTOBIOGRAPHY. ON THE ONE HAND, IT SEEMS LIKE **LAZY WRITING**, NOT TO MENTION VAIN, SELF-INDULGENT--

BUT WHEN YOU CAN SENSE AN ARTIST **DEALING** WITH SOMETHING, SHAPING THEIR ***CATHARSIS*** INTO SOMETHING WORTH SHARING--

--PROVOKING A REACTION, WHETHER + OR −, IN AN AUDIENCE, ESSENTIALLY ADDING THEM INTO THE PROCESS...

WELL, THAT'S **ART**.

ZZZ

35
#173

11 JUNE 10 FRIDAY
THE QUITTER
A BUSY FRIDAY: WORKING ON CASANOVA LETTERING IN THE A.M.

PREPARING FOR A SUPER-ROMANTIC DATE THE NEXT DAY, IN THE AFTERNOON --
CHECKLIST

-- AND GIVING MY NOTICE TO SHELTON THAT EVENING! WHOA!
SEND

THEN MORE CASANOVA, INTO THE A.M.!
DHARBIN, YOU FOOL!
35
#178

12 JUNE 10 SATURDAY
A FINE, FINE START
WE WENT ON A DATE, OUR FIRST DATE. WE RODE THE TRAIN TO A FANCY INDIAN PLACE.

AFTER DINNER WE CAUGHT AN OUTDOOR PERFORMANCE OF "A COMEDY OF ERRORS."
HM I SHOULD'VE BROUGHT A BLANKET--
OH IT'S FINE

AT EXACTLY 7.30, I MET PIE-MAKER AT THE STREET FOR A PRE-ARRANGED PICNIC BASKET (AND BLANKET) SURPRISE DROPOFF
TOM COLLINS, ANYONE?
WELL!
CH-CH
CH-CH

THE PLAY WAS TERRIBLE.
35
#179

14 JUNE 10 MONDAY
FILL-IN: MOM DON'T READ THIS
TRY THIS CLASSIC ON THE LADIES! SUNG TO THE TUNE OF FOREIGNER'S "HOT BLOODED!"
HOT LADY! GONNA GIVE IT TO YOOUUU

TAKE MY PENIS! AND PUT IT RIGHT THROUGH YOOUUU!
THRUST
THRUST

IT'S NOT THAT BIG, BUT IT SURE IS SHAARP!

HOT LADY! HOT LADY!
HUMP
HUMP
35
#181

24 JUNE 10 THURSDAY
100° KUNG FU
SMEK

IT IS NO WONDER I CAN BARELY BREAK 160 POUNDS.

25 JUNE 10 FRIDAY
DOUBLE DATE
WE WENT ON A MOVIE DATE WITH KATE'S FRIENDS NAT AND DEREK--
NICE TO MEET YOU
SHAKE
SHAKE

I USUALLY HATE MEETING NEW PEOPLE, BUT DEREK AND I HAD SOMETHING IN COMMON--
WHAT'D YOU THINK OF THE MOVIE?
I SLEPT THROUGH HALF OF IT!
NICE!
#187

26 JUNE 10 SATURDAY
HI REMEMBER ME?
MAN, I SURE FEEL EXTRA SLUGGISH TODAY.

AW HELL

27 JUNE 10 SUNDAY
PULL UP YOUR NOSE, DHARBIN
DEPRESSION IS A LITTLE EASIER TO BEAT WHEN THINGS ARE GOING WELL...
VOOM
SUXALOT!

BUT ONLY A *LITTLE*.
♪
VOOOO
SUXALOT!

28 JUNE 10 MONDAY
SURPRISE DATE
WE DECIDED TO GRAB SOME DINNER, AND ON A WHIM ENDED UP AT A FANCY RESTAURANT.

BY CHANCE WE ENDED UP AT THE MOST ROMANTIC TABLE, ALTHOUGH I THINK THEY ALL WERE, THAT DAY.
SUE ME.

29 JUNE 10 TUESDAY
KUNG FU REPRISE
I'M NOT CUT OUT FOR WORKING OUT IN A FILTHY SKATE PARK WITH NO A/C IN 100° SUMMER WEATHER--
KOFF
KOFF

DAMN THOUGH, I FEEL PRETTY INVINCIBLE AFTERWARDS, HONESTLY.
HA!
35
#189

30 JUNE 10 WEDNESDAY
THE END OF THE BEGIN
SIX MONTHS GONE! I STARTED IN THE SNOW AND I'M ALREADY IN THE SWEAT!

AS I WRITE THIS, IT'S AUGUST 8 AND I'M TRYING TO BEAT THE DEADLINE FOR A PRINT COLL-ECTION OF THESE STRIPS--
COME ONN DHARBIN, COME ON
DHARBIN I WILL STAB YOU IN THE NUTS--

IT'S WEIRD HOW YOU COBBLE TOGETHER A LIFE OUT OF SO MANY DISPARATE LITTLE BITS.
DONE!
I'M GONNA GO SCAN THIS--YOU WORK ON CASANOVA
I'M ON IT!

BUT IT WORKS OK, SOMETIMES.
JEEZ I HATE THAT GUY...
35
#190

2 JULY 10 FRIDAY
SECRET MESSAGE
DID YOU GET THE MESSAGE I HID IN MY LAST HEROES HOTLINE?*
WHAT? WELL LOOK AGAIN!
NO IT'S IN PLAIN VIEW
WELL I CAN'T JUST TELL YOU!

GET YOUR HEAD IN THE GAME, GIRL.

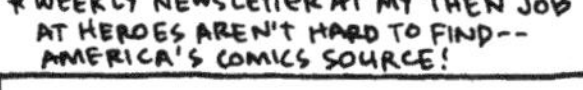
* WEEKLY NEWSLETTER AT MY THEN JOB AT HEROES AREN'T HARD TO FIND-- AMERICA'S COMICS SOURCE!

3 JULY 10 SATURDAY
JULY 4th DATE PREP
LOOKING FOR VEGETARIAN PICNIC IDEAS--
HMM.. PASTA SALAD, BEAN SALAD, IS THAT IT?
SKRITCH
SKRATCH

I GUESS YOU'RE SUPPOSED TO JUST GRAZE A GOOD BIT TOO--
VEGETARIA
SIX BEAN SALAD!!
BS
#192

9 JULY 10 FRIDAY
HOTLINE TRAINING
TEACHING SHAWN AT HEROES HOW TO CODE AND SEND THE WEEKLY NEWSLETTER--
..ANND DONE!
THAT TOOK FOREVER, HUH?

NO, IT'S PRETTY MUCH LIKE THAT EVERY WEEK.

10 JULY 10 SATURDAY
ANNE KOYAMA
SOMEWHERE AROUND THIS TIME ANNE KOYAMA ASKED TO PUBLISH A BOOK BY ME--
AWESOME! JUST LET ME CHECK WITH CHRIS PITZER
TAK TAK
TAK TAK

CHRIS PITZER IS COMICS FAMILY AND I'M VERY LOYAL TO HIM. ONE OF THE BEST, THAT GUY.
HE SAID:
? ? ? ?
OKAY, SURE.
35
#196

19 JULY 10 MONDAY
TAX EVASIVE
I'D GOTTEN A LETTER SAYING I'D FORGOTTEN TO FILE MY STATE TAXES IN 2008 AND NOW OH BOY WAS I IN TROUBLE--

I WENT TO HEROES TO WORK ON SOME STUFF, HELPING THEM TRANSITION OUT OF THE DHARB ERA
SHELTON SAID:
DON'T SWEAT TOO HARD--ONCE YOU FILE THE RETURN IT'LL BE A LOT BETTER
YEAH THAT'S WHAT KATE SAID TOO--I HOPE YOU GUYS ARE RIGHT...
TAK TAK TAK
TAK TAK

SO ARE YOU GUYS DATING OR WHAT? YOU'RE ALWAYS SO EVASIVE...
WELL
WE SPEND A LOT OF TIME TOGETHER AND WE GO ON DATES..
HMPH

SURPRISE! CARSTEN SHOWED UP WITH A CUSTOM-SCREENED SHIRT WITH A BIG TOOTH ON IT!
JUST LIKE IN YOUR COMICS!
I HEART IT SO MUCH!
REAL SHIRT
MADE-UP SHIRT

20 JULY 10 TUESDAY
IDHARBITY CRISIS
AT THE FARMERS' MARKET--
...I SAW THIS HOT GUY OUT OF THE CORNER OF MY EYE AND I WAS LIKE, "OH MY GOD!!!"
HMPH!

BUT THEN I REALIZED IT WAS YOU!
HMPH!
FTW!

21 JULY 10 WEDNESDAY
A DREAM WITHIN A ZZZZ
--SO NOW WE GO INTO THE THIRD DREAM--
--I DON'T UNDERSTAND, WILL YOU EXPLAIN IT TO ME SLOWLY AND THOROUGHLY--
--OF COURSE!

...SO THEN I'LL DO THIS AND THIS, BUT HERE'S SOME BACK
HOW TORTURED A
IFE IS CRAZY A
JESUS, HOW LONG IS THIS MOVIE?
IS IT TOMORROW YET?
PHOOEY!
35
#200

22 JULY 10 THURSDAY
BUDDY LOVE
SOMETIMES MY DOG IS SO CUTE IT MAKES ME SAD INSTEAD OF HAPPY.

HE'S ONLY 5 OR SO, BUT I'M CONSUMED WITH THE IDEA OF HIS LITTLE DOGGIE MORTALITY.
YES, BUDDY
YOU'RE MY GOOD BOY
?
?
?

23 JULY 10 FRIDAY
ENTROPY ALWAYS WINS
SOMETIMES YOU SEE DEPRESSION COMING AND YOU TRY TO OUTRACE IT--

BUT IT'S HARD TO RUN FROM ANYTHING WHEN YOU SIT IN FRONT OF A COMPUTER ALL DAY.
AW HELL

24 JULY 10 SATURDAY
A DEAL WITH THE DHARBIN
SOMETIMES I CAN TURN OFF MY DEPRESSION FOR A LITTLE BIT--
JUST AN HOUR OR TWO, OK?

KATE'S NIECE WAS IN TOWN TO VISIT, AND I WANTED TO BE, WELL, AN ASSET--
TEAM JACOB, HUH?
YEP.
WHAT ARE YOU GUYS' TEAM COLORS?
HUH?

I MEAN, YOU'RE NOT REALLY TURNING IT OFF, I GUESS-- JUST SQUELCHING IT.
YOU GUYS ARE GETTING ICE CREAM? SURE, COUNT ME IN!

IT'S NOT LOSING, BUT IT'S NOT WINNING EITHER.

25 JULY 10 SUNDAY
CATCHING UP IS HARD
SUPER-DUPER
BEHIND!

26 JULY 10 MONDAY
AT SKETCH CLUB, LISTENING TO DEPECHE MODE WHILE DYLAN SETS UP HIS 4×5 CAMERA.
IT'S EVEN BETTER THAN I REMEMBER!
MFRM WRR!
SNAP

27 JULY 10 TUESDAY
AT THE FARMER'S MARKET, I ALWAYS FEEL LIKE I NEED TO EXPLAIN WHY I BAG ALL MY STUFF SEPARATELY--
IT'S FOR MY DOG'S POOPS!
UH-HUH
BEEP BEEP!

28 JULY 10 WEDNESDAY
STIIILLLL
BEHIND!
35
#203

29 JULY 10 THURSDAY
SEXY DATE TALK
I LOVE CUCUMBERS, BUT--
THEY MAKE YOU BURP LIKE CRAZY!
WHAT?
WHAT?

I'VE NEVER NOTICED THIS, AND I SAY SO--
I'VE NEVER NOTICED THIS!
OH, EVERY-ONE KNOWS!
WELL IT DOESN'T AFFECT ME!

BUT LATER, OVER DRINKS--
BURP CLOUD
ROMANTIC TALK
COME A LITTLE CLOSER
HELD-IN BURP!

OH, DHARBIN.
???

31 JULY 10 SATURDAY
JULY JULY
IN MY NOTES FOR TODAY, I HAVE DOWN "CELEBRATION DATE."

BUT I DON'T REMEMBER WHAT THAT MEANS. I DO KNOW THAT IT INVOLVES THIS LADY HERE:

WE DID THIS SO MANY TIMES IN JULY, SOMETIMES PLANNED, SOMETIMES NOT.

BUT THEY WERE ALL GOOD.
GOOD WORK, JULY. GOOD ON YOU.
35
#206

1 AUGUST 10 SUNDAY
RADIO CRAZIES
NPR IS THE WORST ABOUT THIS IDEA OF JOURNALISTIC "BALANCE," ESPECIALLY ON THE WEEKENDS--
--AND THAT'S HOW SCIENCE WORKS--

-- ON THE OTHER HAND, HERE'S WHAT A COMPLETE LUNATIC THINKS--

2 AUGUST 10 MONDAY
IT'S EVEN WORSE WHEN THERE'S A CORPORATION INVOLVED:
--ESTIMATE 50,000 BARRELS PER DAY.

-- BUT BP REPRESENTATIVES SAY "OH NO, 5000 BARRELS TOPS, EVERYONE RELAX, JUST TRUST US, OKAY?"
WHAT'D I MISS, BUDDY?
35
#207

11 AUGUST 10 WEDNESDAY
YES, THE FIRST ONE
AT KATE'S, WATCHING "MAN ON WIRE"--
THIS GUY IS SUCH A DOUCHE
HEY

TELL ME IF THIS BIKINI IS TOO SEXY FOR THAT POOL PARTY..
UT

WHAT ABOUT THIS ONE?
POP!
OH

OKAY THE FIRST ONE THEN.
SURE, WHICHEVER.
36
#212

9 AUGUST 10 MONDAY
MORE WEE HOUR WILLIES
DEADLINE PRESSURE IS PRETTY MUCH ALL YOUR FAULT.

ESPECIALLY SINCE, REMEMBER THIS, EARLIER TODAY?
PEW
PEW

10 AUGUST 10 TUESDAY
BUT IN THE WEE HOURS, YOU JUST GOT TO PUSH ON. EXCUSES NEVER DO ANYONE ANY GOOD.
HM

ALTHOUGH THE LACK OF SLEEP MAKES IT EASY TO FREAK OUT AT FOUR IN THE MORNING.
HMM
TAP TAP TAP
36
#211

13 AUGUST 10 FRIDAY
WHITE WEDDING TALK
AT THE ENGAGEMENT POOL PARTY FOR JOEY AND KATELYN:
SO HAVE YOU SET A DATE YET?
...

IT WAS A "WHITE" PARTY; WE ALL WORE WHITE CLOTHES.
SORRY JOEY-- DUMB QUESTION. I KNOW YOU'RE PROBABLY SICK OF HEARING IT 1,000 TIMES.
IT'S OKAY.

...
...
SKRCH
SKRCH

WHAT ELSE DO YOU ASK A DUDE GETTING MARRIED THOUGH?
I DON'T KNOW-- HOW ABOUT MOVIES, DO YOU LIKE THOSE?
36
#214

16 AUGUST 10 MONDAY
DRAWING ANXIETY
I'VE BEEN HAVING THIS TAX ISSUE THAT'S BEEN GIVING ME SUPER ANXIETY.

17 AUGUST 10 TUESDAY
BUT HOW DO YOU DRAW ANXIETY?
I MEAN, IT'S NOT THE SAME AS JUST WORRYING.

18 AUGUST 10 WEDNESDAY
IT'S LIKE YOUR HEAD IS AT ONCE SMALLER AND BIGGER.
ARE YOU READY TO GO?

YEAH LET ME GET MY STUFF
ARE YOU FEELING OKAY?
36
#216

27 AUGUST 10 FRIDAY
MY BABY, MY BEAUTIFUL BABY
DIARY COMICS #1, FRESH FROM CHINA HERSELF!

IT LOOKS SO GOOD TOO! GOOD WORK CHINA, YOU'RE THE BEST!

28 AUGUST 10 SATURDAY
BUT GETTING BACK TO ME...
I GOT INTERVIEWED BY OUR LOCAL PAPER AT A LOCAL BAR!
SO HOW LONG HAVE YOU BEEN MAKING YOUR OWN COMICS?
HIC
WELL...

YOUR NEW BOOK LOOKS
I KNOW, RIGHT?
HIC
SPILL!
36
#220

29 AUGUST 10 SUNDAY
POOR PRIORITY PARADE
NEVER FAILS, THE MORE WORK I HAVE TO DO, THE MORE DISTRACTING IDEAS I'LL GET--
HMM

BESIDES, THIS DINING ROOM TABLE WAS A WASTE OF MONEY
HRK
--ANYWAY
S-SKOOT

WHAT? IT'S TEN ALREADY?
HECK I'M TOO TIRED TO WORK NOW!

PEW
PEW
#221

30 AUGUST 10 MONDAY
FILL-IN FLASH FORWARD
I DIDN'T HAVE NOTES FOR TODAY. DOES THAT MEAN THAT AUGUST 30 NEVER HAPPENED?
FSHHHHHHH

NORMALLY I'D GO TO BED, BUT IT'S RAINING OUTSIDE AND THE WINDOW'S OPEN AND BITCHES BREW JUST CAME ON RANDOM. LATE NIGHT PLEASURES.
FFSSSSSHHH

SO PLEASANT-- MAKES IT EASY TO STAY UP LATE CATCHING UP ON THESE STRIPS.
STILL NEED AN IDEA THOUGH--
HM MAYBE I'LL ASK TWITTER.
TAKTAK TAKATA

OH MAN THESE ARE TERRIBLE IDEAS.
SLRP
FSHHH
D 36
#222

I SEPTEMBER 10 WEDNESDAY
PUBLIC RELATIONS
YOUR BOOK LOOKS GREAT!
OH THANK YOU!

AND YOUR PUBLISHER DOESN'T EVEN TAKE A CUT?
PRETTY MUCH!
SWEET

I LIKE HOW THESE FIRST ONES ARE ALL CRAPPY.
!

WELL HERE LOOK AT THESE ONES IN THE MIDDLE SEE I NEVER REALLY THOUGHT ABOUT MAKING THEM LOOK GOOD IT WAS JUST AN EXERCISE
36
#224

2 SEPTEMBER 10 THURSDAY
NO BLAME ME
WE HAD A LATE DINNER AND MISSED OUR FRIEND HANNAH'S ART OPENING.
LET'S BLAME ME.
NO, ME-- I'LL TAKE THE BLAME.

SO SORRY WE'RE LATE, HANNAH-- IT WAS MY FAULT
THAT'S OKAY.

NO IT WAS MY FAULT, HANNAH.

#225

3 SEPTEMBER 10 FRIDAY
THE GUILT IS INSIDE YOU
MY DAD'S BUILDING ME A COMBINATION TRAVEL & DISPLAY STAND FOR SHOWS.
BOX UNFOLDS TO FORM THE BASE! IT'S AMAZING!

I HAD GIVEN MY DAD DETAILED PLANS, BUT HE HAD LOTS OF QUESTIONS--
DID YOU GET THAT TEAM VIEW YET?*
NO, DAD
* SOME WEB THING. MY DAD'S LIKE A COMPUTER EXPERT NOW (IN HIS MIND).

WELL I GUESS I KNOW HOW TO GET YOU ON THE PHONE NOW-- JUST WAIT TIL YOU NEED SOMETHING.
AW DAD, DON'T BE PUTTIN A GUILT TRIP ON ME.

OH, THAT GUILT WAS ALREADY IN YOU, I DIDN'T HAVE TO PUT IT ANYWHERE.
ZING!
36
#226

6 SEPTEMBER 10 MONDAY
BIRTHDAY MOM PRESSURE
MY 36th BIRTHDAY! KATE CUT MY HAIR FOR ME. SOUNDS BORING, BUT IT'S ONE OF MY FAVORITE THINGS.
JUST KEEP ME SEXY!
YES YES OKAY
RING RING

HI MOM
THANK YOU VERY MUCH!
KATE IS GIVING ME A HAIRCUT.
SNIP SNIP
YES SHE'S VERY NICE.

SIGH
YES I'M SURE SHE'D LIKE TO MEET YOU TOO, BUT LET'S NOT RUSH IT, OK?
HEE HEE
NO, I KNOW
YES MOM

MOM
HEE HEE
I GET IT, BELIEVE ME, I'M BEING NICE TO HER
SKRICH
YES MOM JEEEZ
36
#229

11 SEPTEMBER 10 SATURDAY
SPX DAY ONE: BEGIN!
SPX! AND THE DEBUT OF "DIARY COMICS #1" HOW META!
DIARY COMICS

WE HAD A SUPREME SPOT IN THE ROOM, AND I WAS WITH A CRACK TEAM OF COMICS COMMAND(BR)OS.
SCOTT C.
TASHA HARRIS
BAGEL
RYAN PEQUIN

FOR ONCE I'D NOT OVERINDULGED THE NIGHT BEFORE, SO I WAS SLEEPY, BUT NOT HUNGOVER.
CAN I DRAW IN THIS FOR YOU?

PLUS SITTING NEXT TO RYAN AND BAGEL WAS PRETTY GREAT--
IS THAT SUPPOSED TO BE ME?
YOUR NOSE IS A PENIS BRO!
HEE HEE!

12 SEPTEMBER 10 SUNDAY
SPX DAY TWO: LET'S DO IT!
ANOTHER MORNING SANS HANGOVER! GUYS I REALLY RECOMMEND IT AT CONS.
HER NAME WAS LOLA

BAGEL AND I EXPLORED BOUNDARIES IN OUR HOTEL ROOM BEFORE THE SHOW.
SKWEERTPTH
FART BARRIER BROKEN, BRO, SORRY
S'OKAY, BRO

ON THE CON FLOOR, SOMEHOW MY SALES WERE EVEN BETTER THAN ON DAY ONE!! (??)!!
WHAT CAN I DRAW IN THIS FOR YOU?
AND YOU
AND YOU
AND YOU

YESSIREE, BEING AWAKE AND NOT ABOUT TO BARF REALLY CHANGES YOUR OUTLOOK, GUYS.
OKAY I GOT YOU ON MY LIST!
STEVE
JENNY
DYLAN
36
#239

12 SEPTEMBER 10 SUNDAY
WOMEN IN COMICS
THAT AFTERNOON I MODERATED A PANEL ON KATE BEATON AND JULIA WERTZ.

REALLY GREAT TO BE PART OF A CONVERSATION WITH TWO YOUNG ARTISTS, AMONG THE SMARTEST IN THE BUSINESS--

FOR ONCE I TRIED TO SAY AS LITTLE AS POSSIBLE, RATHER THAN MY USUAL "TALK OVER EVERY-ONE" STYLE ON PANELS.
NO SWEAT

BUT DON'T WORRY: I GOT MY FOOT IN MY MOUTH NO PROBLEM ANYHOW DURING THE Q&A.
YES, YOU SIR--
YOU MEAN MA'AM?
OH GOD
36
#240

LATER IN THE HOTEL BAR, I DREW MY FAVORITE TINTIN VILLAIN FOR LEIGH WALTON, AND TALKED COMICS WITH SARAH GLIDDEN AND LISA HANAWALT.

13 SEPTEMBER 10 MONDAY
THE LONG GOODBYE
LOTS OF HOTEL LOBBY HUGS AS PEOPLE GET READY TO GO THEIR SEPARATE WAYS.

WELL MEREDITH, I GUESS THIS IS GOODBYE.
OH, I'M SURE WE'LL BE HUGGING AGAIN IN LIKE TEN MINUTES.
PAT PAT

SHE'S RIGHT-- YOU CAN'T LEAVE THESE THINGS UNTIL YOU HUG EVERYONE LIKE FORTY TIMES.
SORRY BOUT THE WAIT, GUYS
OKAY! ALL SET!

WELL MEREDITH, I GUESS THIS IS GOODBYE.
SIGH-H
36
POR MER

13 SEPTEMBER 10 MONDAY
HOME, DHARB, AND STEP ON IT
I DROVE BAGEL AND SCOTT TO THE DC BUS STATION.
..YEAH LIKE WHEN THEY ████ ████ ████* HITLER IN INGLOURIOUS BASTERDS--
NO I LIKED THAT!
GUYS, SPOILLERSS
*REDACTED!

PHIL AND MARÉ CAME OUT TO MEET US AND HELP WITH LUGGAGE. THEY WERE ALL GOING BACK TO NYC ON A BUS (JEALOUSSS).
BROS!
BRO
BRO
BRO
BRO
NO

WHAT A GREAT WEEKEND. THERE REALLY IS NOTHING BETTER THAN THE COMMUNITY I'M A PART OF AS A CARTOONIST--

WELL, MAYBE ONE THING BETTER--
36
#242

14 SEPTEMBER '10 TUESDAY
NEIGHBORHOOD WATCH
THE DAY AFTER SPX, I WOKE UP TO THIS:
KNOCK KNOCK
BARK BARK BARK BARK BARK BARK
BARK BARK BARK
KNO KNO

SOMEONE BUSTED MY CAR WINDOW!
SOMEONE BUSTED YOUR CAR WINDOW!
ONE OF MY NEIGHBORS

IT WAS TRUE! BUT NOTHING HAD BEEN STOLEN--NOT THAT THERE WAS ANYTHING TO STEAL--
...
DUSTIN, SOMEONE BUSTED YOUR CAR WINDOW!*
* ANOTHER NEIGHBOR

MY NEIGHBORS WERE DUTIFULLY ON THE CASE THOUGH--
BARK BARK B
DID YOU KNOW SOMEONE BUSTED YOUR WINDOW?

IS SEPTEMBER 10 WEDNESDAY
FLASHBACK: REALLY OFFICER?
ONE NIGHT LAST MONTH I GOT PULLED AT 2:30 AM COMING HOME FROM KATE'S...
...IN MY OWN DRIVEWAY.

I HADN'T BEEN DRINKING, BUT I REALLY DIDN'T WANT MY NEIGHBORS TO WAKE UP AND SEE ME "WALKING THE LINE."
I PULLED YOU FOR EXPIRED REGISTRATION.
FEIGNS SURPRISE!

MY CAR WAS A LEMON. LOTS OF DUMB PROBLEMS, AND A LEAK THAT MADE IT STINK LIKE MILDEW, AND IT COULDN'T PASS INSPECTION.
AND IT SAYS HERE YOUR INSPECTION IS TWO YEARS OVERDUE.
YEAH, YOU GOT ME.

FLASH FORWARD: SO BY THE TIME THE WINDOW GOT BUSTED OUT, I WAS ALREADY PLANNING TO DONATE THE CAR TO NPR, TO GET OUT OF THAT EXPIRED INSPECTION TICKET.
I HATE YOU, CAR.
#245

16 SEPTEMBER 10 THURSDAY
THE SLINGS AND ARROWS
TRYING TO SCHEDULE AN APPOINTMENT TO REPLACE MY FAKE TEETH APPLIANCE WITH A BRIDGE--
YES MR. HARBIN IT LOOKS LIKE--

--YOUR INSURANCE WON'T COVER THE BRIDGE--
MR. HARBIN?
ROZ

17 SEPTEMBER 10 FRIDAY
IT'S NICE TO CATCH UP WITH FAMILY.
UNCLE DUSTY
MM
POKE

IT'S REALLY NICE TO CATCH UP WITH FAMILY.
UNCLE DUSTY
UNCLE DUSTY
POKE
POKE
36
#246

22 SEPTEMBER 10 WEDNESDAY
ELROY SUGARTHROAT
MY FRIEND ELROY DID A SOLO SHOW--

BUT HIS A/V MESSED UP.
BLEEP! BLEEP!
BLEEP!

LATER I GAVE HIM SOME COMICS I OWED HIM--
THESE LOOK GREAT--
READING YOUR DIARY COMIC JUST REMINDS ME...

...HOW LITTLE WE SEE EACH OTHER ANYMORE.
AW
AW!
AW!
#248

26 SEPTEMBER 10 SUNDAY
DHARBIN IN THE PAPER
THE PROFILE OF ME IN "THE CHARLOTTE OBSERVER" FINALLY CAME OUT--
I SAW THEY REFERRED TO YOU AS MY "GIRLFRIEND"

KATE AND I WERE, COINCIDENTALLY, HAVING A NICE BRUNCH.
DID THAT FREAK YOU OUT?
YEAH
ONLY A LITTLE.
HA!

AT THIS POINT, KATE AND I ARE GETTING SERIOUS, BUT HAVEN'T YET HAD THE OFFICIAL "TALK."

BUT I'M READY TO, FOR SURE.
OH!
SHOULD I KEEP A COPY OF THE PAPER FOR YOUR MOM?
UH, I DON'T THINK WE'RE THERE YET, BABE
HA HA
BLUSH!
36
#250

5 OCTOBER 10 TUESDAY
ART IS ROMANTIC
KATE AND I HAD A MID-DAY DATE AT THE BECHTLER MUSEUM

AFTERWARDS WE HAD DRINKS IN A FANCY RESTAURANT. I'D BEEN THINKING OF HOW TO ASK HER TO BE MY GIRLFRIEND, BUT I WANTED IT TO BE JUST SO, VERY ROMANTIC.
...
...

BUT INSTEAD I GOT CAUGHT UP IN A SWEET MOMENT--
UM
DO YOU WANNA BE MY GIRLFRIEND?
YES!

--AND THEN HAD NO IDEA WHAT TO DO AFTER THAT--
BEAM!
#256

9 OCTOBER 10 SATURDAY
FLOWER POWER
ON A WHIM I DROVE TO THE FARMER'S MARKET AND BOUGHT KATE SOME FLOWERS.
I'M SURE SHE'LL LOVE THEM.

I'M NOT GENERALLY A FLOWER-BUYER. I ALWAYS THOUGHT IT WAS A LITTLE... EASY, IN TERMS OF ROMANCING--
THAT'LL BE $10.75
SOMEONE'S GETTING LUCKY TONIGHT!
HEE-HEE
LADIES!

-- BUT LORD, THEY SURE CAUSED A STIR WHEREVER I WENT--
HOW COME YOU NEVER BUY ME FLOWERS?!
BUT I--
SWAT!

FELLAS, I'M HERE TO TELLYAS:
FLOWERS? FOR ME??
SQUEE!!
FLOWERS WORK.
36
#259

11 OCTOBER 10 MONDAY
THE LATE BIRD GETS PRICIER WORMS
LOTS TO DO THIS WEEK; I'M FLYING TO SAN FRANCISCO ON FRIDAY.
OOG
RUB RUB

I HOPE I DON'T FORGET TO TELL MY BROTHER IN SAN JOSE -- AN HOUR AWAY -- THAT I'M COMING. OR WAIT UNTIL THE LAST MINUTE.
OH YEAH, DON'T FORGET, DHARB.
PERK
PERK
SPOILER ALERT: I DO!

12 OCTOBER 10 TUESDAY
ANOTHER THING I LEFT TIL THE LAST MINUTE IS SHIPPING A BOX OF BOOKS TO S.F. FROM HEROES.
THIRTY POUNDS, THAT'S NOT BAD.
TO APE
LET'S SEE, THAT'LL COST --

SHOULDA DONE THAT LAST WEEK, DHARBIN. COME ON, DUDE.
SIXTY BUCKS?!
PLOP!
TO APE
B 36 #261

10 OCTOBER 10 SUNDAY
OH AT LEAST 24-HOUR SOUR
HAVING A FIGHT IN THE WEE HOURS IS TERRIBLE.
BUT BUT BUT--

AND YOU SAY EVEN DUMBER STUFF THAN NORMAL BECAUSE YOU'RE HALF-ASLEEP--
I THINK YOU JUST WANT TO BE MAD!

THEN IN THE MORNING, YOU'VE HAD NO SLEEP AND YOUR HEART WANTS TO BARF--

ON THE OTHER HAND, IF YOU MAKE UP THAT VERY DAY, ONLY ONE 24-HOUR PERIOD IS RUINED!
NO, I'M TOTALLY STUPID. TOTALLY.
YES, YOU TOO.
YEAH, I'M BASICALLY DEAD ON MY FEET.
Z
36
#260

13 OCTOBER 10 WEDNESDAY
PREPARAPETIONS (GET IT?)
DOING CONS IS ALWAYS A CRAPSHOOT AS FAR AS FINANCIAL VIABILITY GOES--
OKAY PLUS THE SHIPPING PLUS A CHECKED BAG, PLUS FOOD, PLUS TRAIN-FARE, PLUS MORE FOOD, PLUS BOOZE, OH JEEZ
TAP TAP

I COULD NEVER HAVE AFFORDED TO GO TO A.P.E. (ALTERNATIVE PRESS EXPO) WITHOUT ANNE KOYAMA'S SUPPORT. OH, AND ALSO GABE MILLER'S HOSPITALITY.
OKAY THE BIZZAROS ARE GETTING BUDDY, AND DYLAN WILL FEED KITTY, AND KATE'LL DRIVE TO THE AIRPORT AT SIX, LET'S SEE, THAT TRANSFER MIGHT NOT GO THROUGH, BETTER STOP AT THE BANK--

14 OCTOBER 10 THURSDAY
THE DAY BEFORE I LEFT, THEY CAME TO TAKE MY SAAB TO THE NPR JUNKYARD IN THE SKY.
SKWEEK!
SKWEEEK
VAYA CON DIOS, SAAB!

THAT NIGHT I SLEPT OVER AT KATE'S, SO IT WOULD BE EASIER TO GET TO THE AIRPORT EARLY--
I SET IT FOR 5.15.
GASP!!
ZZZ

15 OCTOBER 10 FRIDAY
DOUCHEBAG IN SEAT 13-C
ON THE PLANE TO SAN FRANCISCO, AND APE:
COMPLETE WITH COMPLIMENTARY DOUCHEBAG:
YEAH, THERE'S A LOTTA LIGHT LOAFERS ON THIS PLANE.

THERE'S ONE ON EVERY PLANE!
NO I MEAN, YOU KNOW--LIGHT IN THE LOAFERS.
NO, LIKE, THEY'RE GAY

I CAN'T SLEEP ON PLANES FOR SOME WEIRD REASON. EVEN AFTER THE TERROR SUBSIDES.
OH YEAH, I GOT TONS OF MONEY, LOTS OF MONEY.
YEAH, US MECHANICS MAKE, LIKE, TONS.

GOOD THING TOO!
YEAH I'M GONNA CHECK ME OUT SOME WEST COAST TALENT, KNOW 'M' SAY'N'?
HAHA YEEAHH
GIRLS, I MEAN GIRLS.
36
#263

15 OCTOBER 10 FRIDAY
AIR TERRORS
WHEN FLYING THROUGH CLOUDS TO LAND, I ALWAYS IMAGINE CRASHING.
LIKE, WHAT WOULD IT BE LIKE?
AW MAN

WOULD WE HAVE TIME TO REACT, BEFORE THE PLANE BROKE APART?

OR WOULD IT BE INSTANTANEOUS, WITH NO CHANCE TO... ANYTHING?
CRAS

FORTUNATELY--
SKRT!
D
36
#264

15 OCTOBER 10 FRIDAY
APE: HELLO SAN FRANCISCO
COMING INTO SAN FRANCISCO ON THE TRAIN. **MOUNTAINS** IN THE **CITY**!
...
...

I GOT TO GABE'S BUILDING AND WAITED TO MEET HIM IN THE POSH FOYER--
...

HIS APARTMENT IS **SMACK** IN THE MIDDLE OF THE CITY. UBER POSH.
YEAH, NOT A BAD VIEW, HUH?
...

GABE'S **CORGI** AND I SPOKE THE SAME LANGUAGE--
TRUMAN'S AFRAID OF **DUDES**.
WE'RE **ROOMIES** NOW, TRUMAN!
...
36
#265

15 OCTOBER 10 FRIDAY
DHARBLE FINE

GABE AND I WENT BACK TO HIS WORK, AT **DOUBLE FINE**, WHERE I WAS REUNITED WITH SOME **DOUBLE BROS**--

BRO!

¡GIGGLE!¡

TASHA!

SCOTT!

A NEW BRO!

IF I'M NERVOUS ABOUT MEETING SOMEONE AND WANT TO IMPRESS THEM, CHANCES ARE *1000%* THAT I'LL BUNG IT UP SOMEHOW--

16 OCTOBER 10 SATURDAY
APE : DAY ONE
DAY ONE STARTS OUT SLOW AT THE ALTERNATIVE PRESS EXPO!
...

I WAS SET UP NEXT TO DOUBLE FINE IN THE CHEAP SEATS, AT THE BACK OF THE HALL.
I WON'T LIE, I WAS GETTING NERVOUS.
SCRATCH
SCRATCH

LATER TIM SCHAFER SHOWED UP. SITTING NEXT TO HIM FOR TWO HOURS WAS PURE PLEASURE.
WHAT ARE YOU SIGNING WITH? SHARPIE?
WELL I DON'T REALLY SIGN A LOT.
YOU'LL GET THERE

INEXPLICABLY, I BOUGHT AN ORIGINAL POPEYE WATERCOLOR BY TOM NEELY THAT I'D BEEN DROOLING OVER FOR YEARS.
$100
HOW CAN I PASS UP A BARGAIN?
IT'S NO WONDER I'M BROKE.

16 OCTOBER 10 SATURDAY
SLEEPY TIME PIRATE BAR
WE LEFT THE ISOTOPE PARTY AND HIT UP THIS PIRATE-THEMED BAR THE GUYS KNEW--
TCH TCH

IT WAS COOL, BUT DUSTY-POO WAS GETTING PRETTY SLEEPY-PIE.
LOOK AT ALL THESE RUMS-- I DON'T KNOW WHERE TO START!
AVAST!

WE'RE GOOD DUDES, SO WE WAITED FOR GABE TO SOBER UP BEFORE HE VESPA-ED HOME.
WHEN WE GET HOME YOU GOTTA SEE THE ROOF OF MY BUILDING!
OH UM
Z

BUT HE WAS RIGHT:
TOLD YOU!
!!

16 OCTOBER 10 SATURDAY
EGGS, PHONES, COMMODES
AFTER THE SHOW WE WENT TO A FANCY RESTAURANT WITH FANCIER DRINKS--
A COCKTAIL WITH EGG? I'LL TAKE IT!
OH ESS
EGGGG

MY PHONE WASN'T WORKING THOUGH, AND I WAS MISSING KATE.
I JUST HAVE TO TELL HER ABOUT THIS WHISKEY SOUR!
SEND SEND SEND

LATER WE WENT TO THIS FAMOUS COMICS SHOP, "ISOTOPE," WHICH HAD DRAWN-ON TOILET SEATS ALL OVER THE WALLS.

THERE WAS FREE BOOZE, A LINE 100-DEEP FOR THE BAR, AND TOILET SEATS EVERYWHERE.
LET'S GET OUT OF HERE
I FEEL LIKE I'M IN AN AIRPORT BATHROOM.
36
#269

17 OCTOBER 10 SUNDAY
APE: DAY TWO ANOMALY
BY SUNDAY MY SALES WERE AT A POINT WHERE I COULD RELAX A LITTLE.

A FEW TABLES DOWN FROM ME WAS A TABLE SELLING JACK CHICK TRACTS. I GREW UP ON THEM.
BABYLON
THE MORMON THREAT
ANTICHRI

THEY'RE HATEFUL, EVIL LITTLE THINGS; THEY'RE LIKE EVERYTHING WRONG WITH RELIGION, EXCEPT IN COMICS FORM.
HATE
GAY MENACE
ROCK

I FELT REPULSED AND QUEASY TO BE SO NEAR THEM.
GAY
CHIC
#271

10 OCTOBER 10 MONDAY
FRISCO'S INNER BEAUTY
THE NEXT MORNING I GOT UP EARLY TO WALK AROUND SAN FRANCISCO A LITTLE

IT'S A WEIRD PLACE. LOTS OF OLD BUILDINGS SMUSHED UP NEXT TO UGLY NEW ONES.

LIKE A NEW CITY IS SPROUTING OUT OF THE OLD ONE, SQUEEZING UP THROUGH ANY CRACK IT CAN FIND.
DING DING

NATURE ABHORS A VACUUM.
36

18 OCTOBER 10 MONDAY
SAN FRANCISCO SPEED TRIALS
BY THE TIME THE MOMA OPENED, I ONLY HAD A HALF-HOUR LEFT TO CRUISE IT--
KLK

I HAD TO CATCH A PLANE BACK HOME TO NORTH CACK-A-LACK.
KLK KLK
KLK

BUT THEN I GOT SLOWED DOWN WHEN I FOUND AN ARCHITECTURAL BOOKSTORE--
HM KATE WOULD LOVE THIS BOOK, TOO...
FANCY SPACE

THEN I GOT SLOWED DOWN SAYING GOODBYE TO TRUMAN--
Dear Gabe--
Ur dog is in
♡ w/me
SPLURP
HAHA
GUCKA
#275

18 OCTOBER 10 MONDAY
THANK YOU AIRTRAN
SO OF COURSE I WAS LATE TO THE TRAIN TO THE AIRPORT--
NO NO NO NO NO
TO SFO
BART
TRUNDLE

CARRYING AROUND A TON OF HEAVY COMICS CRAP MAKES FOR SOME SWEATY STRESS.
30 MINUTES TO DEPARTURE, OHHH
COME ONNN

BUT, BIZARRELY, THE AIRTRAN ATTENDANTS WERE INSANELY POLITE AND HELPFUL--
WE'LL HAVE TO CHECK YOUR BAG FOR FREE AND ESCORT YOU TO THE FRONT OF SECURITY IF WE'RE GONNA GET YOU ON THIS PLANE!
PLOP!

AMAZING! ON THE PLANE, NO EXTRA CHARGE, READY TO FLY!
I ALMOST DIDN'T MAKE IT!
36
#276

22 OCTOBER 10 FRIDAY
LET THE BAD AIR OUT, DHARB
I'D SPENT ALL WEEK DRIVING MYSELF COO-COO TRYING TO FINISH A PAID STRIP.
UNGH
MMFFF
CLK CLK TAP TIP TOP

LIKE EVERYTHING, I GOT WAY TOO COMPLICATED WITH IT. BUT I GOT IT DONE, IT LOOKED GOOD, I TOOK OFF MY FLIGHT HELMET, GAZED MEANINGFULLY INTO THE CAMERAS AND SAID:
MISSION ACCOMPLISHED!
KRK
KRK
SEND

KATE AND I WENT OUT FOR A NICE DINNER. IT ALWAYS TAKES ME A LITTLE WHILE TO LET THE STRESS GO.
ARE YOU READY TO ORD--
WHAT? YES? WATER?
??
300 EAST

WHEN IT FINALLY GOES, IT FEELS SO GOOOOOOODDD--
AAAAAH
36
#278

26 OCTOBER 10 TUESDAY
DHARBIN OF THE WINDS
WALKING HOME FROM KUNG FU, UNDER A POSSIBLE TORNADO THREAT--

I WAS RACING THE STORM, WITH MY SORE LEGS AND SWEATY NECK. THE INDIAN SUMMER WIND WAS WARM AND STRONG AND ERRATIC.

I FELT LIKE A GOD.

LATER, MY BODY REMINDED ME THAT I WAS NOT.
36
#281

29 OCTOBER 10 FRIDAY
GET IT TOGETHER, DHARBIN
IF YOU'RE ALWAYS BEHIND ON DEADLINES (LIKE ME), IT'S PROBABLY YOUR OWN FAULT.

IT DOESN'T HELP WHEN YOU GET THAT OLE DEPRESSION ON TOP OF DEADLINE STRESS--
AW DAMMIT

IT JUST MAKES IT EASIER TO BE LIKE "OH WOE IS ME," ETC. LIKE YOU WERE DOING EVERYTHING RIGHT OTHERWISE.

WHATEVER, DHARBIN.
PULL UP YOUR UNDIES AND QUIT WHINING.
YEAH, SERIOUSLY
#282

30 OCTOBER 10 SATURDAY
BIRDS ARE NOTORIOUSLY IMMODEST
KATE AND I DRESSED UP AS BIRDS FOR THE FIRST OF TWO HALLOWEEN NIGHTS--

DYLAN CAME OVER AND TOOK SOME FANCY PHOTOS OF US. KATE KEPT TRYING TO HAVE ACCIDENTAL COSTUME MALFUNCTIONS--
WOULD YOU CUT IT OUT!
UH OH
NIPPP SLIPP
!
SHIMMY

KATE IS AN EXTRAORDINARY, EXCITING, BEAUTIFUL WOMAN, THE KIND MOST MEN WILL NEVER BE LUCKY ENOUGH TO KNOW--

WHAT DID I DO TO DESERVE SUCH A WOMAN?
UH-OH NIPPPP SLIPPP
KATE!
SHIMMY!
D
36
#283

31 OCTOBER 10 SUNDAY
ALL FOXES' EVE
ON HALLOWEEN ITSELF, WE DRESSED AS FOXES, BUT OUR COSTUMES WERE A LITTLE LESS... RIGHT.
ESPECIALLY MINE.

I HAD BEEN STRUGGLING WITH A DEEP DEPRESSION ALL WEEK, AND IT WAS HARD TO GET EXCITED ABOUT BEING SOCIAL. FACTS OF LIFE.

BEING AROUND KATE ALWAYS HELPS THOUGH. SHE'S PRETTY GREAT.
WE DON'T HAVE TO DO ANYTHING SPECIAL-- LET'S JUST SIT AND CHAT, JUST US.

I HOPE I'M EVEN HALF AS GOOD FOR HER--
IT'S TRUE, YOUR MASK DOES LOOK A LITTLE RAT-ISH.
GASP! YOU SAID IT WAS FINE!
DID I SAY THAT?
36
#284

1 NOVEMBER 10 MONDAY
HATE THIS DUDE
TRYING TO START THE MONTH RIGHT: FINISHED CASANOVA 5 LETTERS.
NOVEMBER WILL BE THE BEST MONTH
YES, THE BEST!

2 NOVEMBER 10 TUESDAY
BUT I WAS STILL STRUGGLING WITH "OL' SCRATCH"
HURRK
THESE ORDERS ARE GLKK PILING UP!

3 NOVEMBER 10 WEDNESDAY
I WOULD KILL HIM IF I COULD; I WOULD MURDER HIM IN COLD BLOOD.
THESE ORDERS WON'T PACK THEM-SELVES!

4 NOVEMBER 10 THURSDAY
SOMETIMES THE ONLY ANSWER IS JUST TO PUSH ALL THE WAY THROUGH IT, I GUESS?
OFF TO MAIL THESE ORDERS, DOUCHE!

5 NOVEMBER 10 FRIDAY
FILL-IN: JUST RELAXXX
KATE AND I STOPPED BY THIS SEX SHOP. DON'T ASK ME WHY.
OH, RELAX!

IN MY OWN WEIRD WAY, I'M PRETTY UPTIGHT ABOUT SEX STUFF.
THE DESIGN OF ALL THIS PACKAGING IS AWFUL!
SWEETIE, NOBODY CARES ABOUT THE DESIGN.
RIB!

MAYBE KATE'S RIGHT-- MAYBE I SHOULD JUST RELAX--
IS THAT GREY IN YOUR HAIR NATURAL? COS YOU ARE WORKIN' IT!
OH, UH
!

CAN YOU BELIEVE THAT SKANK?
I WAS STANDING RIGHT THERE!
OH, RELAX

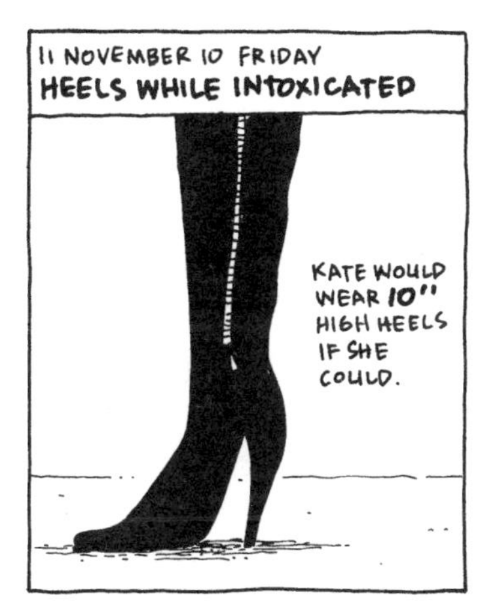
11 NOVEMBER 10 FRIDAY
HEELS WHILE INTOXICATED
KATE WOULD WEAR 10" HIGH HEELS IF SHE COULD.

WE HAD DINNER AND SOME DRINKS UPTOWN. KATE WAS WEARING SOME CRAZY TALL HEELS, AND SHE WAS DRIVING WITH A BUZZ--
LET'S TAKE A PICTURE WITH BILLY ELLIOTT
OOP! YOU GOTTA SLOW DOWN!
BILLY ELLIOT

HA!
WE SHOULD HAVE BEEN IN THIS PLAY!
WE'RE NATURALS!
UT!
FWOOP

BUT NO, NO WE SHOULDN'T HAVE
OH NO ARE YOU OKAY??
ARE YOU LAUGHING IN PAIN?
HA HA HA HA HA HA HA HA HA HA HA HA HA HA
SLIPS AGAIN!
B 36 #289

12 NOVEMBER 10 SATURDAY
FILL-IN: DOOKIE DAY
WINDING UP A DROPCORD IN THE BACKYARD IN THE DARK, I MADE A TERRIBLE DISCOVERY!
!
THERE'S DOOK ON MY HANDS!

WHILE WASHING MY HANDS: ANOTHER TERRIBLE DISCOVERY!
THERE'S DOOK ON MY FEET!
SNF
SNF

AND IN THE BATHTUB!
AAAAH
THERE'S DOOK ON MY FACE!!

TRULY, THERE WAS DOOK ON THAT DAY.
OH SHUTUP.
36
H290

13 NOVEMBER 10 SATURDAY
TALL PEOPLE KISSING
ONE EVENING, DURING A GOODBYE KISS--
HERE LET ME SHOW YOU SOME-THING--

I'LL HAVE TO GET UP HIGHER..
??

I'M GOING TO SHOW YOU WHAT KISSING A TALL PERSON'S LIKE
COME HERE.

READY?
HARD SMOOCH!
36
#291

18 NOVEMBER 10 THURSDAY
DOOK-FUSION
GO AHEAD BUDDY
SNF SNF

THAT'S MY BOY!

HM
HUMP
HUMP
HUMP

THERE YOU, GOOD BOY..
ANY LANDING YOU CAN WALK AWAY FROM
DOOK
DOOK
36
#293

22 NOVEMBER 10 MONDAY
THE DESIGN FLAW IS YOU, DHARB
SO MY DAD BUILT ME THIS DISPLAY CASE AND STAND FOR CONVENTIONS.

FLAT SIDES!
SHELVES SLOT IN!
MODULAR!
CLOSES TO AN APP. 15" CUBE!
HOLDS ABOUT 120 BOOKS!

THE TRICKY PART WAS FIGURING OUT HOW TO PACK IT TIGHT, SO NOTHING WOULD MOVE DURING SHIPPING...
AND SOME BAND-AIDS, JUST IN CASE!

...BUT STILL BE ABLE TO CLOSE IT.
NO NO NO NO C'MON BUTTHOLE
FLUMPH!
36
#295

23 NOVEMBER 10 TUESDAY
A MEMORY OF YORE
IT'S GETTING COLDER!
REMINDS ME OF SOME LIL DHARBIN MEMORIES--
HI THAT IS ME!

MY DAD HAD THESE BATTERY-POWERED SOCKS HE WORE IN THE WINTER TO KEEP HIS FEET WARM.
THESE'RE MY HOT SOCKS!

THEY TOOK FOUR--FOUR--SIZE "D" BATTERIES, AND WERE EXCELLENT FOR BATTLES--
PEW PEW

THEY ALSO INTRODUCED ME TO THE FACT THAT MY DAD'S FEET SMELL AWFUL.
MOM ARE YOU STEAMING CABBAGE?
Z
36
#296

26 NOVEMBER 10 FRIDAY
NEW YORK PLANS
KATE AND I ARE PLANNING A TRIP TO "NEW YORK CITY."
PERHAPS YOU'VE HEARD OF IT?

27 NOVEMBER 10 SATURDAY
WE'RE GOING FOR FIVE DAYS, ONE OF WHICH IS FOR A COMICS SHOW.
...AND MY FAVORITE RESTAURANT BY THE GUGGENHEIM, TWICE!

28 NOVEMBER 10 SUNDAY
KATE'S WORKED OUT AN AGGRESSIVE SCHEDULE, FILLED WITH MUSEUMS AND SHOWS--
SEE? AND THE MUSEUM'S JUST ONE BIG SPIRAL!

29 NOVEMBER 10 MONDAY
MEANWHILE I'M GETTING MY DUCKS IN A ROW FOR THE SHOW-- GOTTA MAKE SOME BENJAMINS Y'ALL.
CARSTEN THEY LOOK GREAT!
NEW SHIRTS!
36
#299

1 DECEMBER 10 WEDNESDAY
BAD NEWS
A COUPLE DAYS BEFORE OUR TRIP, KATE GOT BAD NEWS--HER DOG WAS SICK.
REALLY SICK.
:'(

VIOLET WAS FOURTEEN YEARS OLD, AND AS SWEET A LADY AS YOU COULD IMAGINE, EVEN WITH THE VERY BEST IMAGINATION.
Z

...SO I WON'T BE ABLE TO GO TO NEW YORK--
I HAVE TO STAY HERE WITH HER
OF COURSE. I'M SO SORRY SWEETIE

AND DON'T SEND ME PICTURES OF ALL THE COOL STUFF YOU'RE DOING EITHER!!
!!
36
#299

3 DECEMBER 10 FRIDAY
OFF TO THE AIRPORT
KATE VERY KINDLY GOT UP AND DROVE ME TO THE AIRPORT.
YOU DRIVE.

SHE'D BEEN UP ALL NIGHT WITH HER DOG. I FELT TERRIBLE FOR LEAVING HER IN THE MIDDLE OF A CRISIS.
NOT MUCH TRAFFIC, HUH?

ONE OF MY WEAKNESSES IS BEING TERRIBLE IN SPOTS LIKE THIS; NEVER KNOWING WHEN SOMEONE NEEDS MORE OR JUST FOR ME TO SHUTUP AND SIMPLY BE THERE.
I'M SO SORRY SWEETIE
I'LL MISS YOU
OK

OR NEITHER. BUT, INEVITABLY, I END UP MAKING IT ABOUT ME.
SHUTTLE!
VROOM
36
#302

3 DECEMBER 10 FRIDAY
I ♥ NY
BAGEL GAVE ME SOME SWEET DIRECTIONS TO MANHATTAN, USA.
BROOM BROOOO

I ALWAYS GET MIXED UP WITH THE TRAINS, THOUGH. DID YOU KNOW THEY GO IN TWO DIRECTIONS??
SO THE 4 AND THE 5 ARE THE SAME TRAIN?
FOR YOU, YES.

FORTUNATELY, NEW YORKERS ALL DELIGHT IN GIVING DIRECTIONS.
THANKS GUYS!
NEW YORKERS ARE PRETTY GREAT.

ESPECIALLY THIS GUY--
BAGEL!!!
(APPLAUSE APPLAUSE)
WELCOME TO NEW YORK, EVERYONE!
36
#303

3 DECEMBER 10 FRIDAY
THE BEST LAID PLANS
WE WENT TO BAGEL'S TO GET THE BIG WOODEN BOX I'D SHIPPED HIM.
SURE YOU DON'T NEED HELP, BRO?
NO, YOU GOT WORK TO DO--
I'LL SEE YOU LATER!

BUT I WAS WRONG. APPARENTLY CARRYING 60 POUNDS OF BOX UP 7 FLIGHTS OF STAIRS IS HARD??
3
HRK!

I WAS STAYING WITH SCOTT CAMPBELL, IN HIS EAGLE EYRIE.
GOD WHY?

I NEED A CAREER WITH LIGHTER LUGGAGE--
HUFF HUFF
36
#305

3 DECEMBER 10 FRIDAY
A NEAR MISS
I SAT ON THE COUCH FOR AN HOUR -- THOSE STAIRS HAD REALLY GOTTEN ME.

I THOUGHT SOMETHING WAS WRONG WITH ME; I WAS SO HOT--THEN I REMEMBERED NEW YORK RADIATORS.
I ESCAPED JUST BEFORE A DEPRESSION TOOK HOLD--
NOT THIS WEEK, YOU DEMON!

I WALKED AROUND SCOTT'S NEIGH-BORHOOD AND FOUND A BAR TO DRAW IN WHILE BAGEL FINISHED HIS WORK.
LAPHROAIG, PLEASE
RIGHT
BAR

BY THE TIME BAGEL SHOWED UP, I WAS OUT OF THE WOODS AND HALF IN THE BAG.
LET'S SEE--WHAT ARE YOU HAVING?
HA HA, GOOD ONE!
36
#306

4 DECEMBER 10 FRIDAY
THE BROOKLYN COMICS AND--
--GRAPHICS FESTIVAL! AT LONG LAST, THE WILD PARTY BEGINS!
MEEE

I WAS SITTING WITH "SWEET" ANNE KOYAMA AND FELLOW BROYAMAS MICHAEL DEFORGE AND STEVE MANALE.

PLUS THE WOWEE ZONK BROS--THOUGH MY CHUNKY DISPLAY OBSCURED THEM SOMEWHAT :C
DIARY
DIARY

PRETTY SWEET COMPANY ALL AROUND. ALSO--APPARENTLY TALL PEOPLE ARE SCARCE IN BROOKLYN.
MEEEEEEEEEEE
36
#308

4 DECEMBER 10 SATURDAY
SHORT PEOPLE... UNITE & TAKE OVER
I'VE NEVER DONE A NEW YORK SHOW AS A GUEST BEFORE-- SO I MET A TON OF PEOPLE I'D ONLY KNOWN ONLINE.
BLAH BLAH BLAH
ME ME

SITTING ALONE IN FRONT OF A COMPUTER OR AT A DRAWING BOARD HAS DULLED MY SOCIAL SKILLS--
YOU SEEMED TALLER ON TWITTER!
UM
TOM "SMO" SMOLENSKI

KATE WARNS ME ABOUT THIS ALL THE TIME. I GUESS I CAN BE PRETTY OBLIVIOUS.
HA HA RYAN! YOU AREN'T TALL AT ALL!!
ER
RYAN FLANDERS, MAD MAGAZINE.

AND SLOW TO LEARN.
CINDY!
ISN'T IT CRAZY HOW SHORT EVERYONE ON THE INTERNET IS?
CINDY AU, KICKSTARTER
3/6
#309

4 DECEMBER 10 SATURDAY
THE L IN KIMCHI IS SILENT
THE SHOW WAS BUSY ALL DAY -- I RARELY HAD THE TIME TO GET OUT AND CHAT WITH PEOPLE --
SO IT'S "DOM-UH-TEEL"?
"DOE-MUH-TEEL

I THOUGHT I WOULDN'T HAVE TIME TO EAT, IT WAS SO BUSY-- BUT THERE WAS AN "ASIA DOG" DOWNSTAIRS--
DID SHE SAY "TEEL"? MAYBE I DIDN'T HEAR THE L??
THIS KIMCHI SMELLS FUNKY!

IT WAS MY FIRST KIMCHI! BUT MICHAEL DEFORGE LIKED IT FUNKY! AS FUNKY AS COULD BE!
DUDE YES! THE FUNKIER THE BETTER!
TAKE IT!

LATER I PICKED UP THE BOOKS DOMITILLE HAD SKETCHED IN FOR ME.
I LOVE IT!
DOMI-TEE, RIGHT?
DOMITEE!
DANG IT!
36
#310

4 DECEMBER 10 SATURDAY
YOU ALWAYS HURT THE ONES YOU LOVE
FOR A ONE-DAY SHOW, BROOKLYN WAS A GOOD MONEYMAKER.
I THINK WE ALL DID GOOD?
I KNOW, RIGHT?
ANNE HAS APPLE CHEEKS!

I WAS PRETTY GOOD ABOUT NOT BUYING THINGS, BUT THERE WERE A FEW THINGS I HAD TO HAVE--
TRANS UTOPIA

SAMMY HARKHAM STOPPED BY THE TABLE. ONE OF MY VERY FAVORITES, JUST A FASCINATING ARTIST AND MAN.
I PUT YOU IN A COMIC FROM HEROESCON--
YOU KNOW, ABOUT HOW YOU LOOK SOUR SOMETIMES?
WHAT?

I WAS WORRIED I MIGHT HAVE OFFENDED HIM, BUT--
PFFT
STILL WITH THE AUTOBIO?
DISMISS
DISMISS
#311

4 DECEMBER 10 SATURDAY
DHARBIN JUST SHUT UP ALREADY
AFTER THE SHOW, I WALKED WITH DOMITILLE AND HER FRIEND TO DINNER--
YEAH JUST TELL YOUR FRIEND TO MEET US ALL THERE!

NEW YORKERS ARE ALL SO **FRIENDLY,** THIS GUY **ESPECIALLY** SO.
YOU SHOULD GET A REAL **"NEW YORK MARTINIZING"** WHILE YOU'RE IN TOWN.
ONE HOUR
HA HA, MUCH BETTER THAN THOSE CHICAGO **DEEP DISH** MARTINIZINGS!

NEW YORKERS ARE ALL **POWER WALKERS,** TOO, JEEZ.
I'M SORRY, TELL ME YOUR ~HUFF~ NAME AGAIN?
TUNDE!
PIZZA
TOONDIE?

AFTERWARDS, I FOUND OUT TUNDE WAS **FAMOUS**-- MAKING HIM EVEN MORE LONGSUFFERING IN RETROSPECT.
TONDAY?
TUNDE
TOONDAY?
TUNDE
MENU

4 DECEMBER 10 SATURDAY
COMICAL MASS
IT'S ALWAYS STRANGE AND AMAZING TO BE AROUND TONS OF CARTOONISTS.
DUSTY THIS IS JAMES McSHANE.

WE'RE LARGELY A SOLITARY BUNCH, BY AVOCATION.
WEREN'T YOU IN A KRAMERS ERGOT?
HE WAS IN TWO KRAMERS!

I GET A WARM FEELING BEING AROUND SO MANY BADASSES.
HA HA WEE GUYS I M!GHT BE DRRUNG

AT THE END OF THE NIGHT, HOME TO SCOTT'S SOFA, AND THE GLITTERING LIGHTS OF MANHATTAN.
#314

5 DECEMBER 10 SUNDAY
TWO MORE FOR BRUNCH
I WOKE UP EXHAUSTED, SLIGHTLY HUNGOVER, AND WITH TWO UGLY SURPRISES--
WHAT THE HELL(S)?!
COLD SORES? FEVER BLISTERS? PIMPLES? PALMETTO BUGS?

I ALMOST CANCELLED MY BRUNCH WITH CLIFF CHIANG AND JENNY LEE AT THEIR GORGEOUS BROOKLYN APARTMENT
AND THE ELEVATOR OPENS RIGHT INTO THE ROOM?!
THAT'S RIGHT.

CLIFF AND JENNY ARE THE BEST; TALKING TO THEM IS LIKE "CLASS AND HOSPITALITY 101."
CUTTING THE "VEINS" OUT OF THE ORANGES!

BY THAT EVENING, MY UGLY LITTLE VISITORS WERE GONE-- MYSTERY!
WHERE THE HELL(S)??
BORGEOUS AGAIN!
36
#315

5 DECEMBER 10 SUNDAY
YOUR DRAWING'S WAY NICER
BAGEL AND SCOTT AND I WENT TO A NEIGHBORHOOD BAR TO DRAW--

WE WERE JOINED BY KATE BEATON, AND THEN QUIZZED RELENTLESSLY BY A DRUNKEN JACKET-LOSER.
LIKE THIS ONE?
NO :SCOFF: WAY NICER THAN THAT!
YES, I SEE
PFT

I LOVE THE IDEA OF DRAWING WITH FRIENDS, BUT THEN I ALWAYS GET NERVOUS AND JITTERY.
ESPECIALLY WITH THESE AMAZING GUYS--

STILL, IT'S ALWAYS GOOD TO GET A FEW MORE OF THOSE BAD DRAWINGS OUT OF MY SYSTEM.
36
#316

5 DECEMBER 10 SUNDAY
PLEASED TO MEET YOU
MY FRIEND EMILIE SHOWED UP AND WE ALL WENT FOR DINNER TO THIS TERRIBLE RUSSIAN PLACE.
PLEASED TO MEET YOU
PLEASED TO MEET YOU

IT'S A TRIP SEEING EMILIE IN NEW YORK-- SHE WAS MY FIRST-EVER GIRLFRIEND IN HIGH SCHOOL, DEEP DEEEP IN THE COUNTRY.
I BET YOU NEVER TELL PEOPLE YOU'RE FROM NORTH CAROLINA--
NO WAY!

SHE'S GOOD PEOPLE THOUGH; WE'VE BOTH CHANGED SO MUCH IN 20 YEARS. WHERE DID THE TIME GO?
PARDON ME, I OVERHEARD-- YOU'RE FROM CHARLOTTE? WE'RE FROM STATES-VILLE! JUST WANTED TO SAY HELLO, PLEASED TO MEET YOU.
OH YEAH?
OH PLEASE

BUT IT'S GOOD TO HAVE ORIGINS.
WAIT, DO YOU ALL KNOW EACH OTHER?
NO
WHAT?
36
#317

for Alejanbro ♡♡♡

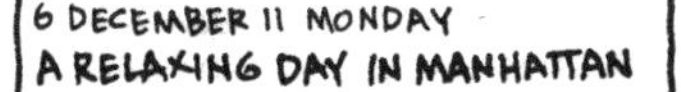

AFTER A STRESS-PACKED HUNT FOR THE **KINOKUNIYA** BOOKSTORE, I MET SCOTT AT THE **MOMA** FOR SOME RELAXING ART VIEWING.

LATER **PHILIP** AND I HAD A RELAXING CHAT IN HIS APARTMENT, THEN BACK OUT INTO THE CITY FOR LIVE **KARAOKE**--

BUT WITH ALL THIS, THE HIGHLIGHT OF THE DAY WAS JUST QUIET CHILLING WITH FRIENDS--

7 DECEMBER 10 TUESDAY
PIZZA ISLAND
SHOULD I GO THIS WAY TO GET TO NASSAU?
I THINK
AIN'T N
SUNS

ON MY LAST DAY IN NYC, I WENT TO PIZZA ISLAND IN BROOKLYN.
THE HINTERLANDS
PIZZA ISLAND!
Here there be Bacon
GREEN POINT LAKE
TO QUEENS
Rent Control Gulch

WORKING IN A STUDIO WITH OTHER CARTOONISTS IS ONE OF MY GREAT UNREQUITED DREAMS IN LIFE.
YOU CAN TAKE THAT LITTLE EMPTY DESK THERE--
IT'S SO CUTE!

SO MUCH OF MY LIFE IS SOLITARY. ALTHOUGH I'M PROBABLY MORE OF A QUICHE ISLAND. OR STROGANOFF.
OKAY!
READY FOR WORK!
#320

7 DECEMBER 10 TUESDAY
D - DAY
I CAN'T OVERSTATE HOW VALUABLE MY FEW HOURS AT PIZZA ISLAND WERE.

IT WAS KATE BEATON WHO, INVITED ME TO VISIT THE STUDIO; AND KATE WHO, INDIRECTLY, PROMPTED ME TO START DOING DIARY COMICS.

...ALTHOUGH AT THE TIME IT WAS JUST A SLOPPY EXERCISE--

A LOT CAN HAPPEN IN A YEAR...

SINCE THEN, DIARY COMICS HAVE BECOME SOMETHING OF ONLY INTERMITTENT VALUE.

ALTHOUGH USUALLY LITTLE MORE THAN A BANAL BOOK OF DAYS.
SINCE THEN, DIARY COMICS HAVE BECOME SOMETHING OF
INTERMITTENT VALUE.

CARTOONING IS A GREAT MEDIUM FOR THOSE WISHING TO CONTEMPLATE NOT ONLY THEIR NAVELS...

...BUT THEIR ANUSES.

BUT MY PARTICULAR BUTT-GAZE HAS DONE SOME GOOD THINGS, ESPECIALLY INTRODUCING ME TO ANNE KOYAMA.

AND I HOPE THEY'VE BEEN OF SOME VALUE TO SOMEONE ELSE, SOMEWHERE.

BUT IT'S TIME TO HANG UP THESE GUYS, AT LEAST AS A REGULAR THING--
POOP

LET'S FACE IT-- LIFE IS RARELY INTERESTING ON A DAILY BASIS.
?
???
SPLUT!

AND, AFTER A YEAR, IT'S TIME TO SET ASIDE WHAT HAS BEEN A VALUABLE **STEPPING STONE**.

ALTHOUGH I'LL STILL DO SOME ONCE IN A WHILE WHEN SOMETHING **INTERESTING** HAPPENS.
!!!
PLOP!
POOT!

BUT FOR **NOW**, I HAVE **REAL** COMICS TO MAKE...

...**IMPORTANT** COMICS.
Fart.
!!
PLOP!
PLOP!
PLOP!

I'M LUCKY TO HAVE THE KIND OF FRIENDS IN COMICS THAT I DO, TO LEARN FROM AND RE-CHARGE BATTERIES WITH.

AND EVEN LUCKIER WITH MY FRIENDS OUTSIDE COMICS.

I AM THE LUCKIEST OF ALL.

NOW LET'S SLEEP.
3.6
#325

16 APRIL 11 SATURDAY
DANGER DANGER DANGER DANG
KATE AND I WERE REAR-ENDED ON THE WAY HOME FROM A PARTY--
POW

IT FELT LIKE WE WERE FLYING, IN THE BAD WAY.

NO ONE WAS HURT.
YOU MADE A NOISE--
A NOISE--?
WHAT KIND OF NOISE?

"I DON'T WANT TO SAY-- IT COULD DAMAGE YOUR MANHOOD--"
WOAHHRRLLUNH
1/2
#326

KATE'S CAR WAS TOWED, AND WE WALKED TO MY HOUSE, HALF A BLOCK AWAY.
MY LEGS WON'T STOP SHAKING
WE'RE SAFE, BABY

WE PLAYED CARDS AND TRIED TO RELAX--
"RUMMY ON THE BOARD--"
WOAHRRLLUNH

IT WAS KATE'S CAR THAT HAD BEEN HIT AND DAMAGED, BUT SHE WAS BEING THE STRONG ONE...

D
A
N
G
E
R
CRASH

GOOD THING, TOO.
WOAHHRRLLUNHH
2/2
#377

23 APRIL 11 SATURDAY
THE ANIMAL INSIDE YOU
ON THE WAY HOME FROM ATHENS WITH CHRIS PITZER AFTER THE FLUKE FESTIVAL:
I SLEPT TERRIBLE LAST NIGHT

YEAH YOU WERE MAKING SOME NOISES--
NOISES?

YEAH
KINDA LIKE THOSE ANIMAL NOISES YOU WERE TALKING ABOUT.

NWOAHRRLLUNHH
#318

28 MAY 11 SATURDAY
I LOVE YOU TOO, MAN
AFTER A SUPER APE SHOW, I RAN INTO A NEIGHBOR WHO'D WORKED ON A MOVIE WITH KATE ONCE.
YEAH, WE'VE BEEN DATING F
WHAT?!

COME'ERE!!
CONGRATULATIONS! SHE'S A GREAT GIRL, WAY TO GO!!
HYULK
PAT PAT

UM
ALEX DID YOU HEAR "ENGAGED?" COS I JUST SAID "DATING."
!

I FEEL WEIRD ABOUT HUGGING NOW--
NO TAKEBACKS!

1 AUGUST 11 MONDAY
THIS IS EVERY MORNING
6.30 AM
COME ON DHARBIN LET'S GO

7.00 AM
OKAY!

7.30 AM

9.00 AM
CHOKE
36
#345

21 AUGUST 11 SUNDAY
KIDS SAY THE DARNEDEST THIGS
BABYSITTING, WATCHING "TANGLED" DURING THE SAD PART--
HUG ME
WHAT'S THAT, LUCY?

HUG ME
AWW!

POOR LUCY, IT'S OKAY!
OF COURSE I'LL HUG YOU!
HMMM
HM?

HUNGRY!
OH!
#347

3 SEPTEMBER 11 SATURDAY
RHAPSODY IN NUDE
KATE BOUGHT ME A MASSAGE, MY FIRST MASSAGE EVER.
WILL I HAVE TO TAKE MY CLOTHES OFF?

I MIGHT BE A LITTLE BIT OF A NEVER-NUDE, MAYBE.
KATE SAID I COULD KEEP MY UNDERWEAR ON KATE SAID I

ALSO THE IDEA OF BEING TOUCHED BY STRANGERS-- OR TOUCHED BY ANYONE, REALLY.... BRRR.
HI MY NAME IS
CAN I KEEP MY UNDERWEAR ON??

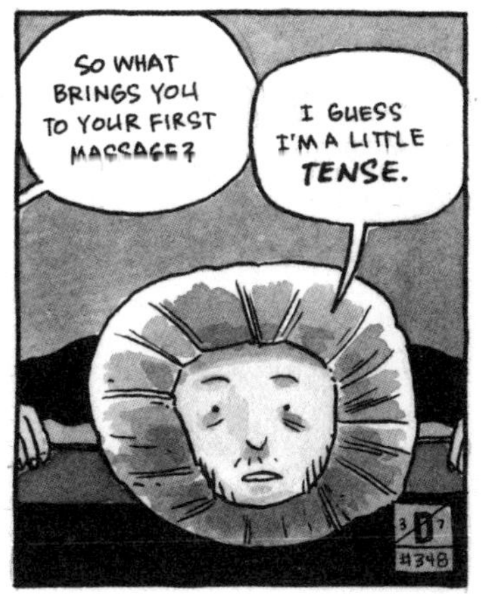
SO WHAT BRINGS YOU TO YOUR FIRST MASSAGE?
I GUESS I'M A LITTLE TENSE.
#348

9 SEPTEMBER 11 FRIDAY
SPX: YOIKS AND AWAY!
SPX AGAIN! GOOD THING TOO-- I WAS TWO MONTHS BEHIND ON RENT. STRESSSS.
ZIP!
BEEP
VROOM
VROOM

THIS WAS THE FIRST "AWAY" CON KATE WAS ATTENDING WITH ME-- SHE'D HAD A STRESSY WEEK TOO.

WE TOOK THE ROUTE THROUGH THE MOUNTAINS, RELAXING AND TALKING ABOUT HOW GREAT EACH OTHER WAS.
NO YOU ARE
NO YOU ARE

IT'S NICE TO GET OUT OF TOWN.
#349

10 SEPTEMBER 11 SATURDAY
GLOW BLOOD SUGAR
DAY ONE OF SPX GOT OFF TO A GOOD START.
TWO ORIGINALS? WELL OKAY!

SELLING ORIGINAL ART FIRST THING ALWAYS GIVES ME THAT GLOW.
GLOW

THIS FEELING GOES ON TIL ABOUT 3, WHEN I REALIZE I HAVEN'T EATEN YET--
GLOW

AND DON'T FORGET THAT PASTA SALAD EITHER
THANK THE LORD FOR KATE.
GMF
HAVE YOU PEED?
FF
SWEETIE!
#351

10 SEPTEMBER 11 SATURDAY
THE PROBLEM WITH PROPRIETY
I WAS ALL SET TO HOST THE IGNATZ AWARDS WHEN GABBY SCHULZ CALLED ME:
I THOUGHT YOU SHOULD KNOW THAT DYLAN JUST DIED

DYLAN WILLIAMS, THE PUBLISHER OF SPARKPLUG COMICS, HAD BEEN BATTLING LEUKEMIA QUIETLY FOR SOME TIME--
I CAN'T JUST GO OUT THERE AND PRETEND IT HASN'T HAPPENED, AND TELLING A BUNCH OF JOKES IS DISRESPECTFUL

NOBODY KNEW WHAT TO DO. THE ORGANIZERS HAD THEIR OWN PRIORITIES. MINUTES BEFORE WE STARTED, I FOUND TOM NEELY AND HE SET ME STRAIGHT--
MOST PEOPLE STILL DON'T KNOW, AND THIS ISN'T HOW THEY SHOULD FIND OUT.
YOU'RE RIGHT

THANK YOU TOM NEELY.
CLAP
CLAP
#353

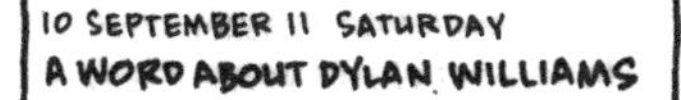

I WASN'T CLOSE TO DYLAN WILLIAMS, BUT I KNEW AND LIKED HIM--

HE WAS A KIND OF RARITY IN THE COMICS WORLD. HE TOOK HIMSELF AND HIS WORK SERIOUSLY, AND HE WALKED HIS TALK-- DYLAN PUBLISHED THE COMICS THAT HE WANTED TO SEE IN THE WORLD.

I HOPE WHEN I DIE, I'LL BE REMEMBERED AS DYLAN HAS BEEN--

-- AS MUCH FOR THE THINGS HE ADDED TO THE WORLD AS FOR THE SPACE HE LEFT BEHIND.

10 SEPTEMBER 11 SATURDAY
BRICKS WERE THROWN
THE IGNATZ WENT FINE, EXCEPT THAT THE SOUND SYSTEM DUDE DIDN'T KNOW HOW TO WORK...
... THE SOUND SYSTEM.
ROXX
KCH
ANNN

OR: THE ENGLISH LANGUAGE:
YES! YOU HEAR?
ROKKKSSSS
KRCH
ANN

BUMMER. I SPENT A LOT OF TIME MAKING MUSIC CUES FOR ALL THE PRESENTERS--
LADIES AND GENTLEMEN: MR. CHESTER BROWN
RROXXXANNNE

MAYBE FOR THE BEST, THOUGH-- I REALLY LOVE CHESTER BROWN; I'D HATE TO OFFEND HIM JUST FOR THE SAKE OF AWARD SHOW PATTER.
OOOHH
KABLOUIS-RIEL!
#355

10 SEPTEMBER 11 SATURDAY
DHARB KNOTTS
AFTER THE IGNATZ PARTY, WE ENDED UP IN A HOTEL ROOM, AS USUAL. I'M STILL NOT GOOD AT CONVERSATIONS.
HEY CAN I ASK YOU A QUESTION? WHY DO YOU WRITE LIKE A BORED TEENAGER?

TRUTH SERUM WORKS BOTH WAYS.
I MEAN, DON'T TAKE THAT THE WRONG WAY.
WHERE IS THIS GOING?

BOOZE TURNS ME INTO A CONVERSATIONAL DON KNOTTS.
HEY ARE YOU TED MAY? I LOVE YOUR COMICS!
NO I'M JESSE FUCHS!

AS OPPOSED TO "REGULAR" DON KNOTTS.
ARE YOU SURE?
PRETTY SURE.
HEY DUSTIN IS THAT GUY WITH THE GUITAR WITH YOU?
#356

11 SEPTEMBER 11 SUNDAY
THE MIRACLE OF LUNCH
DAY TWO OF SPX! GOOD THING I DIDN'T DRINK TOO MUCH LAST NIGHT!
HERE BABE, I BOUGHT YOU A SANDWICH

WOW BRO, THAT SANDWICH IS HUGE!
... YES BRO.
YOU WANT SOME?

WHERE DID IT COME FROM
IT'S HUGE
IT'S SO GREASY
KATE BROUGHT IT
I KNOW IT'S PERFECT
WHOA
OH MAN
GLORF

D
31
#357

11 SEPTEMBER 2011 SUNDAY
DHARBIE STRESSBUCKS
AFTER SPX, WE ALL WENT OUT FOR A QUASI-SURPRISE BIRTHDAY DINNER FOR ERIC FEURSTEIN--
AFTER DINNER WE CAN STEAL THE DECLARATION OF INDEPENDENCE

ANNE KOYAMA HAD GIVEN ME SOME MONEY TO BUY A FEW PEOPLE DINNER ON HER BUT--
OOPS
I FORGOT THE HOTEL DOES THAT CREDIT HOLD THING-- MY ACCOUNT'S ALL LOCKED UP

I HAD A 2ND CARD WITH ABOUT $200 ON IT, SO AS LONG AS THE TAB STAYED UNDER THAT I WAS OK.
WHAT NOW?
I CAN'T TELL WHAT BRIAN IS ORDERING.

IT WORKED OUT, BUT IN MY RELIEF I DID THE MATH WRONG AND OVERTIPPED LIKE CRAZY.
OH THANK YOU! THANK YOU SIR!
UH-OH
#358

11 SEPTEMBER 11 SUNDAY
LEAST INTIMIDATING JOB EVER
THE HOTEL BAR CLOSED, SO WE FOUND A COMFY NOOK TO PLAY MIKE MITCHELL'S **DRAWING** GAME--
OKAY, NOW DRAW **SNORLAX**!

THE HOTEL STAFF WAS **SUSPICIOUS**.
Y'ALL CAN'T BE DOWN HERE DRINKING AND MAKING A **MESS** NOW
DON'T WORRY SIR-- WE'RE JUST CARTOONISTS PLAYING A **DRAWING** GAME--

ALLLL RIGHT
CARTOONISTS: LEAST DANGEROUS DEMO-GRAPHIC **EVER**!
NOW DRAW UNCLE SCROOGE!
#359

12 SEPTEMBER 11 MONDAY
TRAIN IN VAIN
THE NEXT MORNING WE GAVE SOME FRIENDS A RIDE TO THE TRAIN STATION--
BYE BYE
BYE
HUG HUG
SHOULDN'T HAVE HAD BREAKFAST, SHOULDN'T HAVE HAD BREAKFAST

I MAY HAVE UNDER-ESTIMATED HOW LONG IT WOULD TAKE TO GET INTO WASHINGTON D.C. PROPER--
HA-HA THERE SURE ARE A LOT OF STOPLIGHTS HUH?

AT LEAST ONE TOO MANY:
DUSTIN THE LIGHT
HUH WH--
OH SHHHII-
I GOT THIS
???
ZIP!!

WE MISSED THE TRAIN.
D
37
#360

31 DECEMBER 11 SATURDAY
TERMINAL DREAMS
IN MY DREAMS THINGS ARE ALWAYS TERMINAL.
WHA?
MY TOOTH FELL OUT!

THERE'S ONLY A TINY SPACE BETWEEN NOTICING A PROBLEM--
PEW
PEW
AAAAHH ALL MY TEEF AW FAWBIN OWD!!
NOOOO

--AND ITS EXPLOSION.
NOOOOOO

NNN
NNO
#362

SOME SCIENTISTS THINK DREAMS ARE YOUR BRAIN PRACTICING.
PANT OH GOD YES
STILL THERE PANT

I LOVE THIS IDEA, ALTHOUGH I ALMOST NEVER REMEMBER MY DREAMS.

HMMM

MY BRAIN IS HIDING ITS PESSIMISM FROM ME.
HMM
#363

24 MARCH 2012 SATURDAY
UNTETHERED
SO MY GIRLFRIEND AND I BROKE UP A FEW WEEKS AGO.
I THINK THAT'S IT FOR THIS LOAD

WE STILL LOVE EACH OTHER; WE'RE STILL VERY MUCH FRIENDS. EVEN BETTER FRIENDS, IN A WAY.
OKAY I'LL TEXT YOU TOMORROW

WHICH HELPS.
#366

WE CONNECT WITH THE WORLD THROUGH OUR SENSES AND THOSE OF THE PEOPLE AROUND US.

YES GOOD BOY--

LET'S GO OUTSIDE

BUT THAT DOESN'T MAKE IT EASY.
BARK?

#368

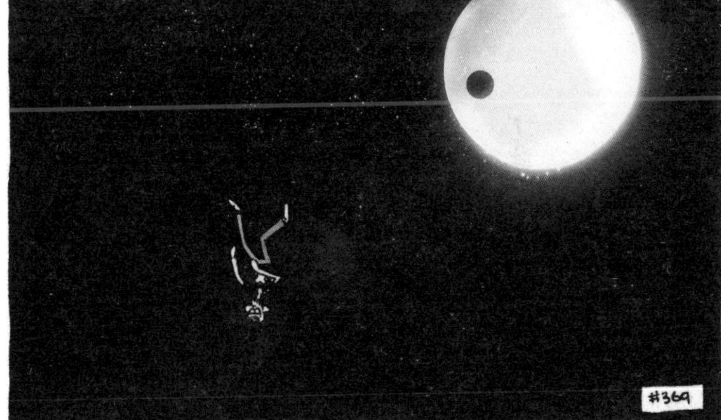
#369

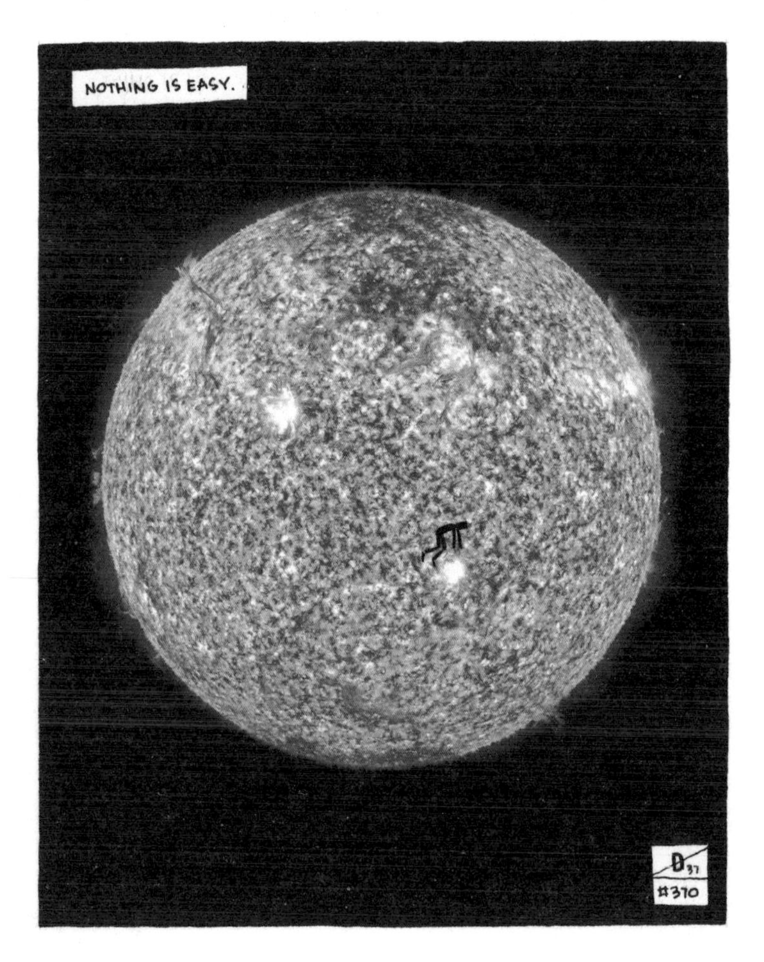
NOTHING IS EASY.
#370

16 APRIL 12 MONDAY
SITREP
How are you?

ow are you?
Tired, alone, desperate, daily sinking in an ocean of weariness with no bott
FIP
FIP
FIP
FIP

bout 8.
Okay.
ow are you?
Tired, alone, des
FUP
FUP
FUP

bout 8.
Okay.
ow are you?
Fine :)
D
#371

HEMBY BRIDGE

1 JUNE 2012
BOXES, PT 1
S-SKR-TCH

OH!
HI THERE, REMEMBER ME?

IT'S BEEN A WHILE, I KNOW--
I'VE BEEN BUSY WITH WORK STUFF..

...AND ALSO SOME BUMMER STUFF.
WOE IS MEEE
OH THE HUMANITY
SORRY BOUT THAT. IT'S BEEN A BAD YEAR.
#372

OF COURSE, IF YOU READ THIS COMIC RIGHT AFTER EARLIER ENTRIES, RATHER THAN THREE MONTHS LATER...

...THEN NO TIME HAS PASSED AT ALL...

ISN'T THAT WEIRD? TIME WAS THERE, AND THEN IT WASN'T.
OR, IT WAS NEVER "THERE."

DID WE CREATE "TIME"? ME, BY PRESENTING TWO MOMENTS--
!!
#373

-- AND YOU, BY INTERPRETING THEM?

POP!
WHO KNOWS?
JA, HELLO!

IS TIME MERELY A PERCEIVED PHENOMENON, OR IN FACT A FORCE AS REAL AND MUTABLE AS GRAVITY?
SQUIK
SQUIK

ANYWAY, THAT'S NOT WHAT I WANTED TO TALK ABOUT--
WAIT, I WAZN'T--
POP!
#374

*TORONTO COMIC ARTS FESTIVAL

I GO TO CONVENTIONS ALL THE TIME -- I DO ABOUT 4-5 A YEAR.

YOU HAVE A REGULAR LIFE, AND THEN, SUDDENLY, YOU'RE BEHIND A TABLE AGAIN.
HI HOW ARE YOU!

AND THE TIME SINCE THE LAST TABLE HAS COLLAPSED TO ZERO...

--USUALLY HAVING FORGOTTEN THE LESSONS OF PREVIOUS TABLES--
HI HOW ARE? YOU?
#376

LOTS OF MY FAVORITE PEOPLE EITHER LIVE IN TORONTO OR GO TO TCAF--
HEY BRYAN
HEY, DUSTIN

ALTHOUGH I'M STILL NOT VERY GOOD AT TALKING TO ANY OF THEM--
MAN! YOU'RE TALL. HAVE YOU ALWAYS BEEN THAT TALL?
WELL

FORTUNATELY, I DIDN'T HAVE A LOT OF TIME TO TALK TO FRIENDS...
OH WAIT I HAVE SOME CUSTOMERS
WELL

BUT ANYWAY, THAT'S NOT WHAT I WANTED TO TALK ABOUT--
NOW HOLD ON A--
POP
#377

29 JUNE 2012 FRIDAY
BOXES, PT 3
AFTER TCAF ON SATURDAY, I WAS TO PRESENT ONE OF THE DOUG WRIGHT AWARDS, THE "TALENT DESERVING WIDER RECOGNITION" AWARD.*

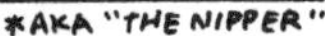
*AKA "THE NIPPER"

I HAD MOST OF A SPEECH WRITTEN, BUT THEN WRIGHT ORGANIZER BRAD MACKAY SAID:
DON'T GO ON ABOUT HOW YOU LOVE US AND ALL THAT

WE DON'T WANT IT TO SEEM LIKE WE IMPORTED SOME AMERICAN TO TELL US HOW GREAT WE ARE.

#378

* POORLY REMEMBERED ** NOT ME THOUGH (NON-CANADIAN)

* FOR AVANT-GARDE/EXPERIMENTAL WORK

I THINK COMICS IS STILL A YOUNG ENOUGH--FLUID ENOUGH--FORM, THAT BOTH STATEMENTS CAN BE TRUE.
--AND THE "NIPPER" FOR TALENT DESERVING WIDER RECOGNITION GOES TO--
--ETHAN RILLY!
CLAP CLAP CLAP CLAP

YOU CAN PUT WHATEVER YOU LIKE IN THE BOX.
NOW WITH AN APPRECIATION OF ETHAN'S WORK, TWO-TIME WRIGHT LOSER, JOHN MARTZ!
YES YES
HAHA

THINGS MEAN WHAT YOU WANT THEM TO MEAN.
AND HE IS THE BEST THE VERY BEST LET TH WORD GO FORTH SHOUT IT FROM THE MOUNTAI TOPS THAT ETHAN IS THE GREATEST IN TH WORLD JUST TH

BUT THAT'S NOT WHAT I WANTED TO TALK ABOUT.
BUT--
DAMMIT!
POP POP

11 JULY 12
BOXES, PT 4
AFTER THE WRIGHTS, SETH INVITED US TO DINNER--

I WAS VERY CAREFUL TO BE COOL ABOUT IT.
JOHN ARE THEY LEAVING? MAYBE WE SHOULD STAND CLOSER JUST IN CASE?
POKE
POKE
POKE

OUTSIDE, AS OUR GROUP SWELLED, JEET HEER WAS CARRYING A BOX.
WHAT'S IN THE BOX, JEET?

IT WAS A BOX OF THE AWARD PROGRAM, WHICH INCLUDED A COMIC I'D DONE ABOUT THEM THE PREVIOUS YEAR--
OH, THIS? IT'S YOU!
#381

IT'S YOU, DUSTIN!

HERE YOU ARE!
OH NO THANK YOU, HA
THRUST!

SETH IS A FAST WALKER.

CHESTER BROWN WAS ON HIS BICYCLE. IT WAS SURREAL, FOLLOWING THESE GUYS AROUND TORONTO IN REAL LIFE.
ARE YOU SURE IT ISN'T LEFT HERE?
#382

THE RESTAURANT WAS LARGE, SPOTLESS, GREEK, AND EMPTY.
LET'S SEE, TWENTY I THINK?

SETH AND CHESTER SAT DOWN AND, SUDDENLY, I WAS NEXT--
WAIT ARE WE SUPPOSED TO SIT, LIKE...
...RIGHT NEXT TO THEM?

HI
HI GUYS

DHARBIN DON'T YO
DHARBIN LISTEN.
DON'T SAY ANYTHING STUPID
#383

I'VE LOST MY CONFIDENCE IN SOCIAL SITUATIONS. ESPECIALLY WHEN THERE ARE CONSEQUENCES--
WELL, AFTER PAYING FOR IT CAME OUT--
NOPE! TOO MANY OPINIONS ABOUT THIS ONE--

I USED TO BE GOOD SOCIALLY, BUT NOW IT'S ALL AN ACT, AND CAN UNRAVEL QUICK IF I'M NOT CAREFUL.
OF COURSE, MY THOUGHTS ON RELIGION HAVE BEEN CHANGING...
NOPE! DEFINITELY COULD GET INTO TROUBLE THERE TOO

I THINK I'VE GOTTEN TO A PLACE WHERE MY MENTAL STATE IS CAUSING REAL DAMAGE TO MY BRAIN.

TO MY EVERYTHING.
WHAT DO YOU THINK, DUSTIN?
KRF
#384

EVEN WITH MY CLOSEST FRIENDS, I'M BARELY ABLE TO COMMUNICATE ANYMORE--
YEAH SO ANYWAY I LIKE IT IT'S GOOD I LIKE GOOD THINGS I'VE HAD A PRETTY BAD YEAR SO YEAH GOOD STUFF IS GOOD

IT'S A SELF-PERPETUATING CYCLE. THE DUMBER THE THINGS I SAY, THE MORE UNCOMFORTABLE I GET ABOUT SAYING ANY NEW THINGS.
swallow

IT MAKES ME RECEDE INWARDS. I END UP ASKING QUESTIONS INSTEAD OF ACTUALLY TALKING.
LIKE I'M HUNTING FOR A THING WE HAVE IN COMMON ANYMORE.
SO, ANOTHER BABY ON THE WAY HUH?
UM

THEY'VE NOTICED.
DO YOU THINK THIS ONE WILL BE MUCH, AH, DIFFERENT?
#385

IT'S NOT THEIR FAULT. THEY'VE ALL GROWN UP, WHILE I'VE BEEN SPINNING WHEELS IN MY VARIOUS FUNKS AND FUGUES.
SPLSH SPLSH

SOMETIMES IT FEELS LIKE I'M WEIRDLY TRYING TO TALK TO YOUNGER VERSIONS OF THEM...

FROM BEFORE MY BRAIN WAS LIKE THIS.

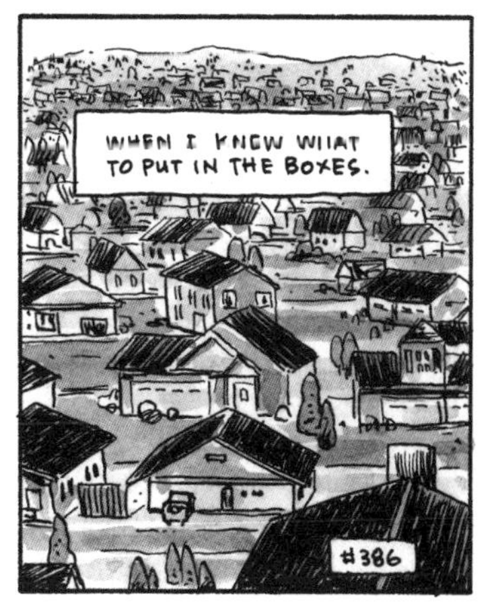
WHEN I KNEW WHAT TO PUT IN THE BOXES.
#386

THINGS DON'T MATTER AS MUCH AS WE THINK.

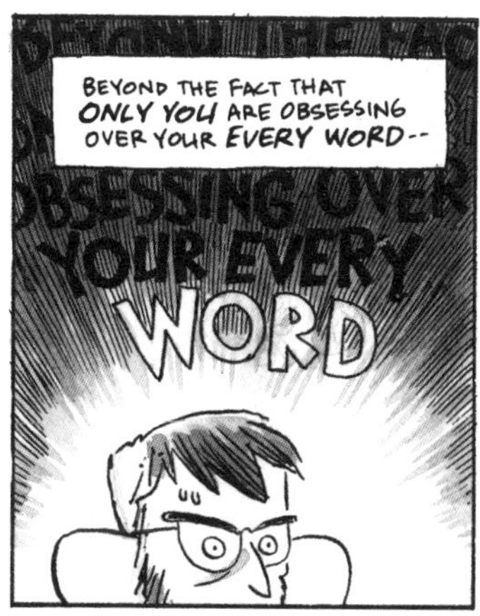
BEYOND THE FACT THAT ONLY YOU ARE OBSESSING OVER YOUR EVERY WORD--
OBSESSING OVER YOUR EVERY WORD

--ULTIMATELY, IT DOESN'T MATTER MUCH ANYWAY.
YOU ARE JUST MEAT, DUSTIN HARBIN!
UM

MEAT, FLOATING THROUGH SPACE!
DUSTIN, DINNER IS NO PLACE FOR METAPHORS!
#390

YOUR HEROES ARE JUST MEAT TOO!
GOD, AMERICANS.

EVEN ALBERT EINSTEIN WAS JUST MEAT!
POP!
JA, HELLO AGAIN!

IT WAS EINSTEIN WHO DECIDED GRAVITY WAS ABOUT THE WORLD AROUND US BEING DEFORMED--
IMAGINE ZPACE IS A GIANT ZOFT MATTRESZ!

"A BODY LIKE ZE EARTH WARPS ZE ZPACE AROUND IT, LIKE A BOWLING BALL ON ZE MATTRESZ--"
#391

"LESZ MASZIVE BODIES ENTER ZIS GRAVITY WELL ARE CAUGHT IN ORBITS DEPENDING ON ZERR OWN RELATIVE MASZ UND VELOCITY.

"MEANWHILE, CREATING THEIR OWN DEPRESSIONZ IN ZE MATTRESZ, PULLING ALONG OTHER, LESSER BODIES.

"ZE EARTH IS TRAPPED BY ZE ZUN, ZE ZUN IS TRAPPED BY ZE MILKY WAY GALAXY, WHICH ZPINS AROUND A ZUPER-MASSIVE BLACK HOLE--

"WHICH IS A ZINGLE GALAXY AMONG MANY MANY TRILLIONS, RACING AWAY EVEN ZTILL FROM ZE ZTUPENDOUS MOMENT OF CREATION.
#392

WE ARE ALL TRAPPED! FLYING THROUGH SPACE!

WE'RE ALL BEING FLUNG AWAY FROM EVERYTHING ELSE AT UNIMAGINABLE SPEEDS--

MOST OF THE TIME WE DON'T NOTICE. OTHER TIMES IT FEELS IMPOSSIBLE NOT TO NOTICE.

AS WE MOVE AWAY FROM EACH OTHER, OUR PERCEIVED WORLDS ARE ALSO ZEPARATING.

"WHAT WAS FORMERLY ROUND AND SCULPTED AND REAL IS NOW JAGGED AND MISSHAPEN AND ALIEN.
#394

OR AT LEAST IT SEEMS THAT WAY. ONLY THE BOX IS NEW.

WE'RE STARING AT THE SAME THING, ONLY NOW IT'S RUSHING AWAY FROM US--

OR MAYBE IT'S WE WHO ARE RUSHING AWAY.
#395

IS ANXIETY JUST OUR BRAIN ZOOMING AWAY FROM ITSELF?

YOU ARE THE SAME: STATIONARY, UNCHANGED. BUT YOUR MIND IS MILLIONS OF LIGHT YEARS AWAY--

POP

--AND ACCELERATING!
#396

WHAT A THING MEANS ISN'T AS IMPORTANT--

--AS WHAT YOU THINK IT MEANS.
#397

POP

ANYWAY--

DINNER WAS GREAT, DESPITE ALL MY BRAIN'S LABORS TO THE CONTRARY.
WHAT A TREAT TO SIT AND CHAT WITH PEOPLE YOU ADMIRE, WHO PROD YOU TO IMPROVE YOURSELF AND
DUSTIN

WE CAN **HEAR** YOU.

AFTER DINNER WE STOOD OUTSIDE TALKING, SLOWLY SEPARATING LIKE PEOPLE DO--

JEET STILL HAD THE BOX FULL OF THE WRIGHT CEREMONY PROGRAMS WITH MY COMIC IN THEM--
YOU GOT SADDLED WITH THAT ALL NIGHT, HUH?

OH THIS?
DO YOU WANT IT?
NO!

NO?
BUT IT'S YOU, DUSTIN!
THRUST!!
#399

THE BOX IS **YOU**!

*PARAPHRASED

ONE THING I'VE LEARNED, IN THE PROCESS OF DOING THESE COMICS, IS THAT I'M ***FAKE,*** VERY FAKE.

SUPER FAKE.

AND I DO THE SAME THING ON THE *INSIDE* AS THE *OUTSIDE*-- I LIVE ALMOST 100% IN MY *HEAD*.

ONE REASON I CAN'T CONNECT TO PEOPLE IS BECAUSE THEY'RE *COMPETING* WITH THE INTERIOR SIMULACRA I'VE CREATED FOR THEM.

IT'S EASY TO FORGET THAT REAL PEOPLE ARE ORGANIC AND UNPREDICTABLE AND CHANGE THEIR MINDS *ALL THE TIME*...

IT WAS A PROBLEM WITH ME AND KATE'S RELATIONSHIP, AND SOMETHING I STILL STRUGGLE WITH.

...EVEN NOW THAT WE'RE BACK TOGETHER.

ONCE WE HAD A FIGHT AND I SAID:
BUT WHAT ABOUT ALL THE SWEET STUFF I SAY IN MY COMICS ABOUT HOW I LOVE YOU?

AND SHE SAID:
I'M SURE THAT'S VERY NICE FOR THAT GIRL BUT I'M A REAL PERSON.
#404

KATE IS SOMEONE WHO SIMPLY LOVES ME, CAN YOU IMAGINE?

I WISH I COULD SAY I FELT MOORED BY THAT, BUT INSTEAD I FEEL ADRIFT, UNSURE HOW I GOT TO THIS PLACE, OR WHY.
#405

WHAT IF THE "REAL" YOU IS THE METAPHOR, AND THE "FAKE" YOU IS THE ONE WITH BONE AND SKIN AND BLOOD AND MUSCLE?

WHAT IF EVERYTHING JUST COMES DOWN TO PUTTING THINGS IN THE RIGHT BOXES, OVER AND OVER, **FOREVER?**

THE **ALTERNATIVE** IS ACCEPTING THE FACT THAT YOU'RE DEEPLY **UNHAPPY**; THAT YOU'RE INCAPABLE OF FIXING IT WITHOUT SOME **VERY** FUNDAMENTAL CHANGES, AND CERTAINLY NOT BY **YOURSELF**.

09

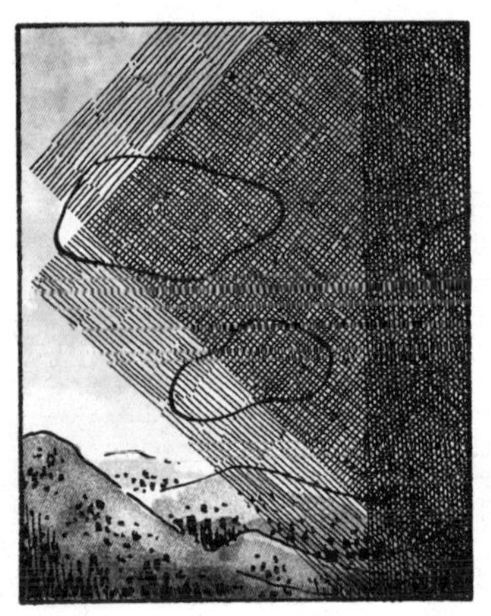

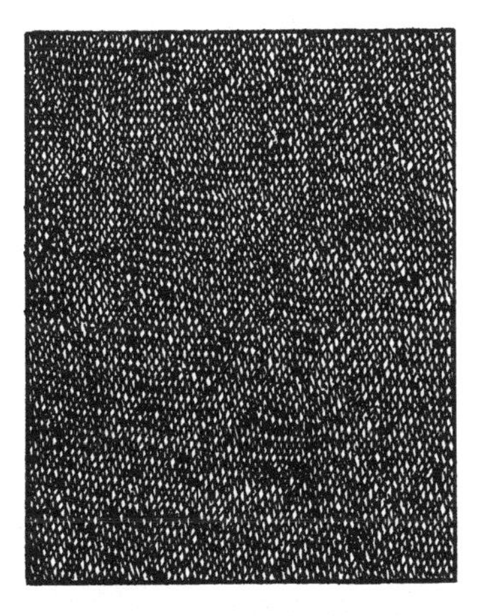

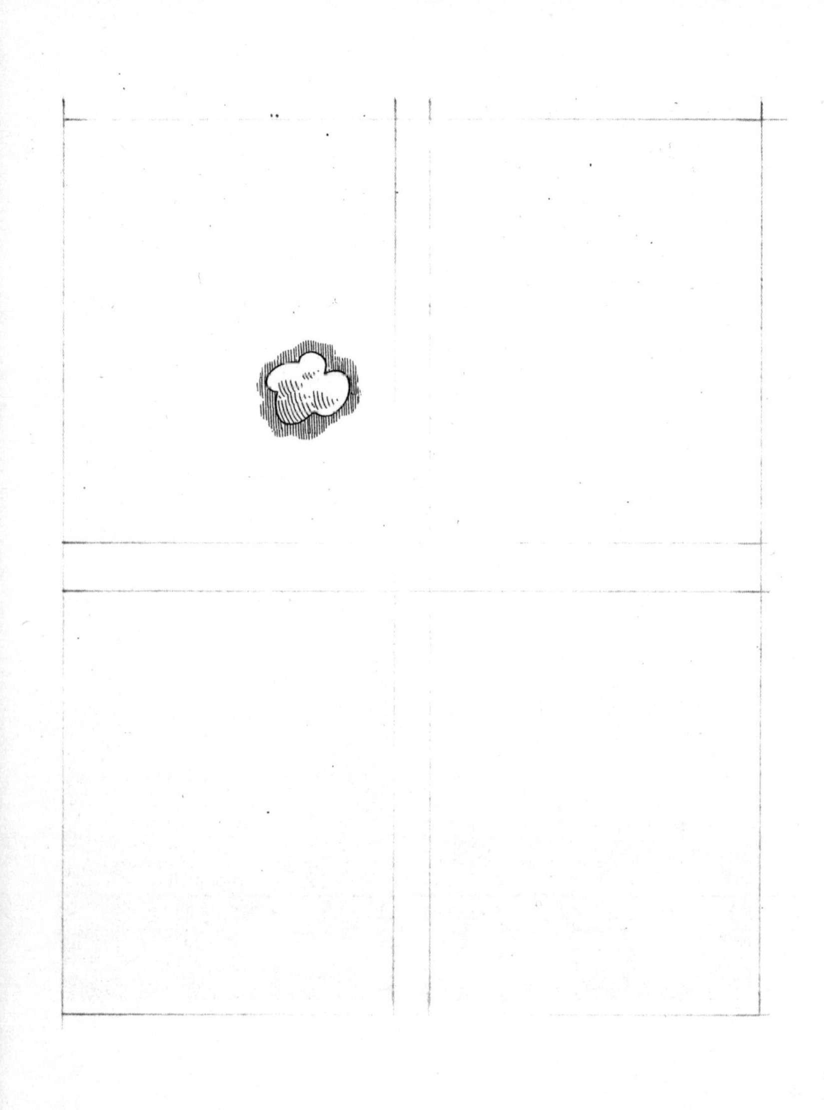

SKCH-KCH
D 39
AUGUST 2015